The Quest for Quality Caring

The Quest for Quality Caring

Improve Your Ability to Relate to Others

Kenneth C. Haugk

Augsburg ■ Minneapolis

THE QUEST FOR QUALITY CARING
Improve Your Ability to Relate to Others

Scripture quotations unless otherwise noted are from the New Revised Standard Version Bible, copyright 1989, Division of Christian Education of the National Council of the Churches of Christ in the United States of America.

Cover design: Lecy Design

Library of Congress Cataloging-in-Publication data

Haugk, Kenneth C., 1945-
    The quest for quality caring : improve your ability to relate to
others / Kenneth C. Haugk.
        p.   cm.
    ISBN 0-8066-2501-5 (alk. paper)
    1. Helping behavior.   2. Interpersonal relations.   I. Title.
BF637.H4H38   1990
158'.2—dc20   90-47490
                                                                   CIP

The paper used in this publication meets the minimum requirements of American National Standard for Information Sciences—Permanence of Paper for Printed Library Materials, ANSI Z329.48-1984.   ∞ ™

Manufactured in the U.S.A.   AF 9-2501

94   93   92   91   90   1   2   3   4   5   6   7   8   9   10

To
Charity and Amity
and to
the quality carer within each of us

Contents

Preface

Storytelling is a proven teaching tool used throughout history and hallowed by Jesus' use of parables to explain eternal truths. "Who is my neighbor?" a lawyer asked, and Jesus responded with the story we call "The Good Samaritan." That story effectively illustrates neighborliness in action.

This book is whimsically presented, but I couldn't be more serious in my purpose: to help readers grow in their ability to care for and relate to others. Discussions about quality caring can easily become abstract and impersonal. This fable of a young koala's quest uses a more personal approach to illustrate practical ways we can grow in caring relationships.

I had fun writing this book! I hope you have just as much fun reading it, because it is intended to appeal to the child in us all. May you read, enjoy, and learn as you pursue your own quest for quality caring.

A Beginning

ONCE UPON A TIME, in a small grove of eucalyptus trees that grew near a spring in Flinders Chase National Park in South Australia, there lived an exceptionally bright young koala named Kalawaka. People would come from all over the world just to get a look at the koalas. Kalawaka never minded, though, because while the people watched the koalas, the koalas watched the people. Learning goes two ways! And of all the koalas, Kalawaka was especially eager to learn. For him, a bus load of tourists was an occasion to add another language to his repertoire. (Although anyone in the know is well acquainted with the fact, many humans seem unaware of the remarkable ability koalas possess for acquiring and retaining new languages.)

When people saw the koalas, they would usually say things like "How cute!" or "How cuddly!" This made all the koalas feel rather proud, including Kalawaka. But one day, as Kalawaka was meditatively dining on eucalyptus leaves, his attention was caught by a little girl who seemed sad and inattentive to the koalas. Instead of watching him and the others, she was picking at the sleeve of her T-shirt and holding back tears. The man who was with her leaned over and murmured, "What's the matter, honey?"

"Oh, Daddy, I miss Mommy. She really liked koalas." Big tears ran down her checks.

Her father picked her up and hugged her tightly. "I know, honey. I was thinking the same thing. I miss her, too." As he held her close, Kalawaka felt tears come into his own eyes. He crept closer on his eucalyptus branch.

"We have each other," the man said. "We have to give each other quality caring. Mommy would want that."

Kalawaka pricked up his ears and stopped his munching. "Quality caring," the man had said. Long after the people had left, he was still musing: *What is "quality caring"?*

Well, that phrase worried him like a pebble in a shoe. It bothered him day and night. He was so curious about things that he just couldn't rest until he understood this new concept. And he worried about whether he was giving other koalas quality caring. (As you may have guessed, Kalawaka was not only bright and eager to learn, but was also very conscientious.)

Kalawaka asked all his friends if they had ever heard about quality caring, but none of them could help him. The phrase kept coming back to him over and over again. One night Kalawaka woke up and shouted, "Enough!" He had made up his mind about what he must do: if the answer couldn't be found in his eucalyptus grove, then he would have to look elsewhere. He had always wanted to travel, and now that he had graduated from school, this would be a great opportunity to see some of the world.

His friends and relatives wept as he said good-bye. Venturing out into the world was, after all, a most un-koalalike thing to do. It had been a tradition of long-standing that the world came to see koalas. No one alive could ever remember it being the other way around. Yet Kalawaka was determined.

Just before he left, his mother handed him a whole bag of the juiciest, chewiest eucalyptus leaves you could ever imagine. His father gave him a present too. "Ka-lawaka," he said (in a tone of voice dads are fond of using on occasions they regard as momentous), "this machine may well help you understand what you find in your search." It was a very modern, portable computer with a data bank stuffed full of the wisdom of the ages. "No modern koala should be without one," he said. "The computer's name is Sophie."

Brushing back the tears from his own eyes, Kalawaka bravely walked away from his eucalyptus grove into the wide world. But the world was a very big place, and Kalawaka was a very small koala. Who could tell him where to begin his quest? The answer was as obvious as the pack on his back. "Why, the computer!" he exclaimed. "Of course!"

Kalawaka thought for a while, sat down, and typed in this question: "Where does a koala start a journey in search of quality caring?"

That should do it! he thought to himself, quite pleased with his own ingenuity. Sophie set to whirring and doing the sort of things computers tend to do when faced with such a challenging question. After probing all her data banks, Sophie flickered this message on the screen:

> Go to Greece, Kalawaka! Start your search in that place of ancient wisdom.

"Greece! Of course!" Kalawaka exclaimed as he stood in line at the Adelaide airport. (Airlines will sell a seat to anyone with a credit card, without blinking an eye.) He settled in for the long trip halfway around the world. As he drifted off to sleep, he wondered again, *Just what is quality caring, anyway?*

Part One

*What Quality
Caring Is*

I want, by understanding myself, to
understand others. I want to be all
that I am capable of becoming. . . .
This all sounds very strenuous and
serious. But now that I have wrestled
with it, it's no longer so. I feel
happy—deep down. *All is well*.
—Katherine Mansfield

1

Genuine

THE PLANE LANDED WITH A JOLT. Kalawaka stretched and
yawned, picked up his precious eucalyptus leaves (and
Sophie) and got off. Any educated koala, even one from
faraway Australia, knows just where to go for advice in
Greece. So Kalawaka got directions, boarded a bus, and
journeyed to the Oracle at Delphi.

In the rugged glen at the base of the mountain, Kalawaka looked around. It was a breezy day—not a cloud
in the sky. Feeling a little unsure of himself, he waited,
wondering what he was supposed to do next.

He must have sat for an hour. Suddenly, he heard—
or at least thought he heard—a whisper in the breeze:
"Know yourself."

Kalawaka jumped. He looked at Sophie. "Did you
hear someone say, 'Know yourself'?" he asked.

No. But it makes good sense. Look into yourself. This is the place to start. Sort your thoughts and feelings; think about what sort of person you really are. Once you know that, accept yourself. Be yourself. You know what happens when you try to be or act like someone else.

Kalawaka knew, all right. He remembered when he was a young koala in school and had decided that all the intelligent koalas were in the chess club. He hated chess with a passion, but he had joined anyway, thinking that everyone would see what a brilliant young koala he was. He had endured those interminable chess meets for a year, but he knew he was bored and miserable. So did everyone else.

Sophie continued as if she knew what he had been remembering:

When you live behind a mask and try to be like someone else, you miss much joy and excitement, feel imprisoned in a role, and even have to lie sometimes.

That's for sure, thought Kalawaka. *All that time I was playing chess I could have played on the soccer team, which I really liked, but I always had to act like I was enjoying myself when I wasn't.* He sighed.

Besides, when you act like someone else, your friends can't enjoy the gift that is you.

"A gift?" Kalawaka exclaimed. "I'm not wearing a bow."

When you know yourself and begin to express your true self, you are on your way to becoming a genuine koala. By acting genuinely you show others how to be themselves too.

"Hmmm," mused Kalawaka. "That's quite profound. I always thought being yourself was no big thing; you just *were*. Maybe it's not that easy."

Some people won't like it when they see you being yourself. Some will secretly envy your personal freedom. Others will feel threatened. But don't let that stop you. After all, the first step in showing genuine care to others is being genuine yourself.

Was it really the Oracle at Delphi who had said, "Know yourself"? Kalawaka didn't know. But that phrase and what Sophie had said about it had given him a great deal to think about. As he sat in the shade of a tree, he knew just what he needed: to munch on some eucalyptus leaves.

After a thoughtful repast, Kalawaka asked Sophie, "How can we summarize what this tells us about quality caring?" He had hardly pushed the "enter" button when Sophie flashed:

Quality caring is genuine.

"Genuine," pondered Kalawaka. "Being really me." He typed a quick "Thanks" into Sophie, who flashed:

Any time!

As he marched back to the road to await the next bus, he felt like a brand-new marsupial.

Rejoice with those who rejoice,
weep with those who weep.
—St. Paul, Romans 12:15

2

Empathic

As the bus bumped along Grecian roads, Kalawaka said aloud, "Well, that was an enlightening experience if there ever was one!" He decided to spend a few more days enjoying Greece, soaking up the sun along the coast. The bus driver dropped him by a perfect inlet, quiet and peaceful, and Kalawaka settled in. He lay there feeling very satisfied with his recently acquired knowledge, and just as he was about to doze off—*SPLASH!* One eye slowly opened and Kalawaka looked around. Up on a pier to his left, a man began calling out loudly to someone in the shallow water by the edge of the pier. Kalawaka sat up and watched the scene.

"That's right, Helen!" the man shouted. "Now, kick hard with your legs. No. No. Don't lift your head out of the water. Turn it to the side. That's right! That's good. Now listen carefully—"

How nice, Kalawaka thought. *He is teaching that little girl to swim.* As the two moved farther down the pier, out of earshot, the only sound to be heard was the rhythmic lapping of the waves along the shore. Kalawaka fell fast asleep and dreamed of—what else?—eucalyptus leaves and his quest.

Some time later, another splash interrupted Kalawaka's peaceful doze. This time, his other eye opened a crack and he surveyed the seascape. Two people had waded into the water. One was an older man. The other was a small boy, maybe six or seven years old. The boy was flailing at the water and kicking, with little success. The man put his arms around the boy to help him stay afloat and guided the boy's limbs through the proper motions. The swimmer then became frightened and cried out, thrashing and choking. But the man was right there, holding him up and helping him along.

Kalawaka watched this spectacle with great fascination. Getting up, he shook the sand out of his fur and headed for Sophie. He typed in all he could remember of the two swimming lessons he had seen: "Sophie, what was so special about the second lesson?" Sophie whirred for a minute, and then once again her screen came to life:

Quality caring is empathic. The first instructor did not get wet; the other did.

Kalawaka scratched his head. "Do you mean getting wet is a way to care better?" he typed.

Let me put it another way. The first instructor only told the girl what to do; the second got in and shared something of the boy's dilemma. To view the world of others from the inside out, to see things from their perspective, is an important step on the road to quality caring. This also communicates your understanding to them, and, consequently, your relationships deepen and your caring shows and grows.

Kalawaka sat back. "Empathy," he said to himself. "Feeling with another. Kind of as if I were in another's place, showing that I understand. I think I see."

How poor are they that have not
patience! What wound did ever
heal but by degrees.
—Shakespeare

3

Patient

As THE SUN BEGAN TO SET, splashing brilliant reds and
purples across the sky, Kalawaka began to think about
finding a place to bed down for the night. With dusk
settling in, he found himself wandering the streets of a
small village, craning his neck every now and then to
view this or that tree. A koala knows how utterly important it is to discover the right tree to sleep in. A down-
home kind of tree means a night of refreshing sleep,
which (as you might have gathered) is considered a
precious commodity among koalas.

Suddenly, out of the gathering darkness, he spotted
a small grove. It was not quite like his grove at home,
but a grove it was nonetheless. As Kalawaka strolled
along, examining one tree after another, he noticed a

number of benches scattered among the trees. Here and there on some of the benches people were seated, speaking with one another or just silently enjoying the stillness of evening. Just then, Kalawaka saw it. "At last," he said to himself. "A perfect tree!"

He climbed up, awkwardly cradling Sophie under his arm. He found a sturdy intersection of three branches and wedged her between them for the night. Just as he settled onto a comfortable branch and prepared for a good night's sleep, he heard voices drawing near his tree. The sound drew closer and Kalawaka could see that two people were walking together. One was taller, but rather bent and wobbly. The other was smaller, but sprightly. Observing them, Kalawaka sensed he was about to learn something about caring. And he had thought he was done for the day. What a bonus!

It was obvious to Kalawaka that the boy could have run far ahead of the old man, but he didn't. Contentedly he walked side-by-side with the man and held his hand. In the semi-darkness Kalawaka could see that the old man was not holding onto the boy; the boy was supporting the man. The scene played out in the twilight beneath the captivated Kalawaka.

The two sat down on the bench under Kalawaka's tree and were silent. At last the old gentleman spoke. "I lived with your grandmother for 57 years, Nikolas."

As they sat, little Nikolas listened, gazing into his grandfather's face. Kalawaka felt he could almost touch the love he saw. During the next half hour, the old man spoke a litany of odds and ends from the scrapbook of his own life, always punctuating them with the refrain: "I lived with your grandmother for 57 years."

Kalawaka could hardly hear the boy's responses, but he could see the upturned face, the motionless body, and the hands clasped about his grandfather's. As they got up to leave, Kalawaka muttered: "My! What a remarkable boy. So well behaved. So patient."

"Patient!" he exclaimed. "That's it! Quality caring is patient, just like that little boy. One who gives quality caring takes time to slow down, walk the pace of an old man, and listen to his story."

Ruefully, Kalawaka recalled the time he had promised to help a young cousin build a model boat to float on the pool in their grove. She was eager to learn but she didn't even know the stern from the bow. Kalawaka went right ahead and put the boat together himself. It turned out to be a nice model boat—but one that Kalawaka built. He remembered that his cousin had played only halfheartedly with the boat. "I guess I needed to learn to wait, to be more patient, like that boy with his grandfather," Kalawaka murmured. "If only I had known then what I know now, I could have worked with my cousin to build her own boat. But it's so hard to be patient sometimes," Kalawaka sighed. "It seems like koalas are awfully busy these days, climbing here and there trying to get everything done by yesterday. I wonder if people have that problem too," he mused.

Kalawaka turned to Sophie. "What can you tell me about patience?" he asked her. Sophie's screen came to life with a warm glow that lit up the surrounding leaves.

Patience is an essential element in caring for others, Kalawaka. Without patience, deep relationships cannot develop. Quality relating takes time and hard work. A patient carer waits and allows a friend to look for his or her own solution—to grow at his or her own rate.

What do you think of that, Kalawaka?

"Wow!"

Where you go, I will go; Where you
lodge I will lodge; your people shall be
my people, and your God my God.
—Ruth, Ruth 1:16

4

Available

THE DAY KALAWAKA ARRIVED IN GERMANY it was bitterly
cold. The wind swept down from the Alpine heights
with such force as to chill a poor koala to the bones.
Kalawaka knew there would be no sleeping out-of-doors
tonight. As uncomfortable as he found beds to be, he
would have to sleep in one. But where in Garmisch–
Partenkirchen would he find a place suited for a koala?
Ah, yes. Perhaps Sophie would know.

And she did. Checking her tie-in to travel agency
software, she directed him to a bed-and-board establishment owned and operated by the Kaiser family.

Homey atmosphere, and the price is right. Sounds ideal for
you, Kalawaka.

When Frau Kaiser answered his knock, she thought that the wind was playing tricks on her. She didn't see a soul. That is, not until Kalawaka managed to shout over the howling wind: "Down here!"

Needless to say, the Kaisers were charmed. What other pension in their town would have such a distinguished foreign guest?

Kalawaka spent the late afternoon thawing out in front of a fire kindled in the massive fireplace and chatting with the other guests. Frau Kaiser was an excellent cook and Herr Kaiser a congenial host. Before the day was done, Kalawaka felt very much a part of the family. In fact, Frau Kaiser even invited him down for a late night snack of kuchen and warm milk.

They had no sooner begun to chat about their respective countries when the telephone rang. Frau Kaiser excused herself and rose to answer it. "Hello. Yes, this is she—Good evening, Marta—No, you're not imposing. I'm pleased to talk with you—Oh, really—Uh huh— Oh—" (Frau Kaiser motioned for Kalawaka to help himself to more kuchen.) "Tell me about what happened— It must have been difficult—What did they say?—How do you feel now, Marta?—Well, you know I am here whenever you need me."

Kalawaka was beginning to feel a bit uncomfortable listening in on what was obviously a private conversation, so he finished another kuchen and retired to the front parlor with his milk. He watched the fire die down until only a few glowing coals remained. Then he took his empty glass back to the kitchen, just in time to hear Frau Kaiser saying, "Call me again whenever you would like—No, just about the only inconvenient time would be when I am tending to breakfast and dinner—Well, thank you, Marta. I love you too—*Wiedersehen!*"

As she hung up the phone, Kalawaka shuffled a little. A pensive Frau Kaiser came over to the table and sat down. "Sorry to interrupt our conversation. That was someone who has been my friend ever since school days. Just six months ago her physician told her she had cancer, and lately she has been feeling worse and worse. She calls me to talk sometimes when she feels down. Oh, she has some very lovely relatives, but I think they are unsure of how to relate to someone so terribly ill. I try to get over to see her every couple of days, but sometimes she just has to talk before then. That's fine by me. She always feels so worried about 'imposing.' Heavens! She is a dear friend. Any time she needs me, I am here. Now, you must tell me more about Australia . . ."

This time Kalawaka did not have to turn to Sophie for information. He saw at once the importance of making oneself available to others.

Love consists in this, that two
solitudes protect and touch and greet
each other.

—Rainer Maria Rilke

5

Present

As the train rumbled across the French heartland toward Paris, the chill of the German Alps melted from Kalawaka's bones. A promising spring met him as he arrived in Paris; it seemed almost like a different world. Tender green shoots sprouted on every tree and shrub and the daffodils burst into explosions of yellow along the roadside. As he surveyed the city from the Eiffel Tower, Kalawaka thought aloud, "This must be the most beautiful city in the world."

After a morning filled with sightseeing, Kalawaka's thoughts turned to food. The food in Germany had convinced him that other things besides eucalyptus leaves could be quite tasty (a significant concession for a koala to make). So Kalawaka decided to enjoy lunch at one of the numerous sidewalk cafés he passed: "Chez Pierre."

The lunch hour was almost over and they were about to stop serving, but such an unusual visitor was accorded special service. He ordered a croissant and café au lait. After serving him, the waiter politely inquired: "Pardon, Monsieur Koala, but we are closing for several hours. Would it inconvenience you to pay now?"

"No, of course not. Here you are."

"Merci, Monsieur! Please feel welcome to sit for as long as you like."

The waiter went on to the next table, where two men were sitting together deep in conversation. Kalawaka took a sip from his coffee and marveled at the warm, gentle breeze. After the waiter departed, the little café became quiet—so quiet that he couldn't help overhearing the conversation at the next table. One man, obviously distressed, was speaking very slowly, his voice charged with an intense sadness. The other followed his words, literally hung on them, and studied his face as he spoke.

Ah, thought Kalawaka, *an opportunity to learn more about caring.* And learn he did!

As he observed the two men, he noticed above all how the one hung on the other's words. It wasn't just that one man was physically there with the other, nor was it that he gave the other his fullest attention. In some manner, it was as if every fiber of the man's being were attuned to that other man and his need. The one was riveted to the other so strongly that Kalawaka wondered if he could touch that thing bonding them together. The incredible sensation of that caring interaction hit Kalawaka like a lightning bolt.

Kalawaka immediately asked Sophie for her reaction. After he typed in his description of the incident, she flashed:

> In quality caring, one is present. There is a saying that goes like this, Kalawaka: "Let there be such a oneness of spirit between you that when the one cries, the other tastes salt."

"You're right, Sophie, That's what I saw today. 'Being present.' Thanks!"

Of all the things he had learned about caring so far on his quest, this one had had the greatest impact. He decided that on the rest of his travels he would be on the lookout for it again and again. He began to realize what a rarity he had witnessed and how fortunate it was that he had witnessed it at all.

Care-fronting is offering genuine
caring that bids another grow. . . .
Care-fronting is offering real
confrontation that calls out new
insight and understanding. . . .
Care-fronting unites love
and power.
—David Augsburger

6

Confrontive

AFTER SPENDING SEVERAL WEEKS touring southern
France and Spain, Kalawaka headed for Great Britain.
He took the ferry from Calais to Folkestone, and his stay
in Britain was both full and delightful. He visited all the
touristy attractions: the changing of the guard at Buck-
ingham Palace, Stratford-on-Avon, and Stonehenge. Yet
he still had plenty of time for rest and relaxation.

The ferry whetted his appetite for the sea. There was
just something special about standing on deck with the
wind ruffling your fur and the tangy salt spray all about
you. So when the time came to move on to the United
States, Kalawaka opted to go by ship. He booked himself
on an ocean liner that was departing from Liverpool in
a week. He arrived in Liverpool a day early. While stroll-
ing around the city, he struck up a conversation with a

gentleman named Alfred. They began to talk about sports. Kalawaka mentioned that he knew a bit about tennis and cricket, but he was always too small to play.

"Oh!" the man said. "Have you ever seen a game of darts? It's quite popular here."

"No, I haven't."

"Well. Are you free this evening?"

"Why yes, I am."

"How would you like to come along with me? My team is playing tonight at the King's Arms on Boswell Street."

"That sounds wonderful," Kalawaka exclaimed.

"I'll meet you there at seven o'clock."

When Kalawaka arrived, Alfred and his teammates were seated around a table.

"Over here, Kalawaka," Alfred called. After the introductions, the conversation resumed. Alfred asked, "Are we all here?"

"No, Captain. Robert is not here yet."

Someone piped in, "Good! Maybe the bloke won't show." That brought a round of "Hear-hear!"

Someone else said, "How did he get on our team, anyway? Could we 'uninvite' him next year?"

"Oh, come on now, he's a good player—got a sharp eye and steady hand."

"Indeed, he does. A shame, though, that he never bothers to pay like the rest of us!"

"Speaking of hands, if he slaps me on the back one more time, I'll—well, he had just better not."

"I know what you mean. I almost hate to make a good throw for fear of his congratulations."

"But gents, you have to admit he is basically a good chap."

"Frankly, I can't take him anymore. And to top it off, he's always late! We almost forfeited the competition last month because of him."

Alfred intervened. "All right, men. Robert's got his faults like the rest of us. Were I in his place, I should prefer that someone speak about them to my face instead of muttering behind my back. What a bunch of magpies! Someone needs to speak to him about a couple of his more unfortunate habits. It's the least we can do before any more talk of booting him off the team."

"Pardon me for saying so, Captain, but I couldn't disagree more. He's not one to take it well—not well at all."

"Maybe not. But wouldn't anyone sooner hear some unpleasantries directly than be dismissed without an explanation?"

"You're right, Captain. And you're the perfect one to do it."

"Now see here," Alfred protested. "How about one of you?" It was no use. A chorus of "Alfred's our man" arose. Alfred glanced at Kalawaka, a little embarrassed. "All right, all right. I'll do it."

And who should arrive just then but Robert. "Evening, chaps. I beg you to excuse my tardiness. But what are we waiting for? Let's begin!"

With glances as deadly as daggers, the game commenced. And, when it was time to pay, Robert happened to be ordering a sandwich. But when Eric scored a bull's-eye, Robert was right there. He whooped, hollered, and slapped Eric on the back so hard that Eric was propelled halfway across the room. The rest of the team members shot Alfred some telling looks, but Alfred smiled an inscrutable little smile and waited.

If someone hit me that hard, Kalawaka thought to himself, *I'd fly from Adelaide to Melbourne.*

Right after the first round, as the team took their break, Kalawaka slipped off the stool where he was perched and made off toward the WC. Out of the corner of his eye he noticed Alfred take Robert by the arm and say, "Robert, my man, I must speak to you for a moment. In private."

Moments later, when Kalawaka emerged, he heard voices around the corner.

"I say, Alfie, you look rather serious."

"Well, it is rather serious, Robert," Alfred said, as they sat down at an empty table. "You know that you are a valued member of our team. Next to Jim Gifford, you are the best thrower we have. But Robert, you have developed some rather irritating habits that, frankly, are coming between you and your teammates."

Robert sputtered and protested, but soon started to laugh. "Come now, Alfie, what did I ever do to any of you chaps?"

"Well, Robert, if you'll hear me out, I'll tell you." It seemed that Robert didn't want to listen, but the grave tone in Alfred's voice was unmistakable. Sounding slightly irritated, Robert responded: "If I have done something that bothers my friends"—his tone was icy—"I want to hear about it. Speak your mind, man."

"Robert, you know we all take turns paying for the game. Many times you don't take your turn. Now it is not just the money that is bothersome, but it says something about what you think of the rest of us." Alfred stopped for a moment.

In the silence Kalawaka could feel Robert's resistance collapsing. He said, "I don't mean to. It just slips my mind—Now that you mention it, I can't recall having paid now for . . . months."

"Robert, I speak for us all: you must remember when it is your turn and pay like the rest of us."

Another silence. After a time Robert breathed deeply and said, "All right, I will try to be more considerate. Anything else?"

"Yes, Robert, a few things more." Robert sat silently. His busy joviality seemed to have disappeared altogether. Alfred went on. "Robert, I know you are an enthusiastic individual. We appreciate it, but you can get carried away. No one enjoys the wallops you deliver when we have a good throw. You make a bad throw almost more welcome than one on target. Frankly, Robert, your wallops hurt."

In a subdued voice, Robert said, "I guess I never thought of it that way, Captain."

"Robert, I'm not saying any of this to make you feel small. It is just that for your good and the good of the team we felt that you should hear these things."

"I understand, Captain. Really. Is that all?"

"One more thing, Robert. Your habitual tardiness must end. A month ago it almost resulted in a forfeit. I suggest you get here on time from now on."

"You've got it, Alfie."

"Oh, that does remind me of just one more thing. My name is not Alfie. It is Alfred. There's only one person on earth I allow to call me Alfie, and that's me mum."

"Yes, Alfi—er, Alfred."

From the noise at the other end of the room, they knew the second game was about to begin. Alfred got up to go back, but Robert stayed put.

"What's the matter, Robert?"

"Captain, I feel—embarrassed, I guess. I don't know if I'm ready to face up to the fellows."

Alfred stretched out a hand to Robert. "Come on, lad," he said softly. "We do want you with us. Otherwise we wouldn't have bothered to say anything to you. We care."

Around the corner, Kalawaka let out his breath. He realized how tightly his paws had been clenched. His shoulders ached from the tension.

"Gracious!" he muttered. "What an encounter! All those difficult things Alfred told him and they are still friends. Maybe that's part of what being a friend is all about. Caring enough to confront someone on difficult things."

Kalawaka knew he'd discovered another important key to quality caring, and he didn't even need Sophie to help him understand what he'd experienced.

So it was that the night before he left Great Britain, Kalawaka learned that quality caring can be confrontive.

And remember, I am with you always,
to the end of the age.
—Jesus, Matthew 28:20

7

Dependable

THE VOYAGE FROM LIVERPOOL to New York was exceptionally relaxing. Kalawaka spent some days organizing
his research and processing data to bring Sophie up-to-
date on his new ideas. Other days he enjoyed playing
deck games or simply sitting back and doing nothing.
When he arrived in the United States, he was quite
refreshed and eager to continue his quest.

He spent the first two weeks touring a few of the more
famous sites along the Eastern Seaboard. He was especially fond of the District of Columbia. Its scores of
monuments and gleaming marble buildings resembling
Greek temples caused him to recall his happy days in
Greece. He was disappointed, however, that not a single
famous koala could be discovered among the multitude

of statues. "Their loss," he murmured to himself. There was more to see than he had time for, so he decided to journey into the heartland of the nation.

As he crossed the United States, he passed through several university towns. There was something different about those towns that he couldn't quite put his paw on. They had a different—for want of a better word—*flavor* than the open countryside or the city. At length his curiosity got the better of him. The next university town he came to, he would stop and spend some time seeing just what made it tick.

The next such town he happened upon was in Indiana, and he was in luck! Graduation had occurred the previous week, so there were many vacant rooms just begging for occupation. The rate being reasonable, Kalawaka decided to stay in the McNutt dormitory.

There were still a number of students around, some living in the dorm and working in town and others awaiting the summer session. Kalawaka soon discovered that the best place to meet people was in the dormitory lounge. There he could sit and chat by the hour.

One evening, as he was sitting there alone reading a travel magazine, two women sat down on the couch across the room. *What a contrast!* Kalawaka thought to himself as he looked up from his magazine. One seemed to be very nervous. She kept wringing her hands and squirming in her seat. The woman at the other end of the couch was as calm as a koala in a cool pool sipping an iced eucalyptus tea. She pulled out a book and began to read. Kalawaka couldn't let the distraught woman sit alone, so he got up, went over, and introduced himself.

"Good evening, my name is Kalawaka."

"Hi . . . uh, I'm Debbie," she said nervously, glancing at her watch and then back to the door. "You're a koala, right?" Kalawaka nodded. "Nice to meet you," she said in a faraway sounding voice.

After a few awkward attempts at conversation, Kalawaka fell silent. Debbie finally spoke again. "Oh, I'm sorry. You must think I'm rude. You see, my boyfriend Jeremy was supposed to meet me here a while ago." She paused."Sometimes he just . . . forgets about our dates. I never really know if he's going to show up until he does."

"Oh," said Kalawaka.

"Don't get me wrong, Kalawaka, I really like him. For a while I found his unpredictability . . . well, exciting, but now . . . now it just . . ."

Kalawaka didn't know what to say. Debbie seemed on the verge of tears. "Poor girl," Kalawaka said to himself as she got up and excused herself to go to the restroom.

Shortly after Debbie left, the woman at the other end of the couch said, "Excuse me, I believe you said your name was Ka—Kawalaka?"

"Close," he said with a smile. "It's Kalawaka."

"Oh! Well, Kalawaka, my name is Susan. You know, it's a real shame how inconsiderate her boyfriend is. I think he likes her. You can tell it when they're together. He just doesn't seem to realize how much his being inconsistent hurts her. My boyfriend Ray certainly isn't perfect, but I can depend on him. When he says he's going to be here, he usually is. If he can't make it, he always tries to call."

Later that evening, after Kalawaka had typed in a complete report, Sophie took almost no time to state the lesson:

Quality caring is dependable. Another word for it might be *reliable*. It is a matter of having respect for others. You saw how Susan benefited from dependable relating, and how Debbie's discomfort was a direct result of a lack of dependability on Jeremy's part.

Kalawaka was reflective as he put Sophie away. There was more to this caring business than he realized. Dependability—another important lesson about caring. He saw that it was time to move on and resolved to take a plane the next morning to Texas.

In this world . . . getting more and
more closely interconnected, we have
to learn to tolerate each other. . . .
—Bertrand Russell

8

Accepting

As Kalawaka settled into his seat on the plane, he
was pleasantly surprised to find a vaguely familiar face
next to him. "Say, aren't you a student at the university?"
he asked.

"Yes, I am," the man answered. "Or was. I graduated
last week. But how did you know that?"

"I stayed several nights in McNutt Hall and saw you
around there. I'm traveling around the world doing research and decided to investigate just what a university
town was like. My name is Kalawaka," he said, extend-
ing his paw.

"Kalawaka, pleased to meet you. I'm Brad Collins."

All the way to Austin, they chatted like old friends.
Brad was very interested in Kalawaka's journey and

made him promise to write whenever he published his notes. The time seemed to fly, and when the pilot asked them to buckle up for the approach to the airport, both were downcast at the prospect of saying good-bye. Suddenly, Brad's face lit up.

"Kalawaka, have you arranged for a place to stay?"

"No. Not yet, at any rate."

"Good. How would you like to stay with my family and me at our ranch?"

Needless to say, Kalawaka was most excited and accepted immediately. A real ranch! It would be just like the Old West picture shows he went to see as a joey. They landed and gathered their baggage and Sophie.

Kalawaka's first clue that he was due for a Texas-sized experience was the astounding proportions of and accoutrements in the car that met them at the airport and took them to the Collins Ranch. The word *stampede* acquired new meaning for Kalawaka as he witnessed Brad's family rushing to greet him with hugs, backslaps, and many a "now don't you look just fine's." Kalawaka felt a little awkward (not to mention unsafe). But as soon as Brad introduced him, they embraced him, too, just as eagerly.

For his return, Brad's parents had planned a surprise party for later that day. When Brad and Kalawaka entered the massive living room that evening, Kalawaka was immediately impressed by the huge cake in the center. A banner at one end of the room read: WELCOME HOME, BRAD. CONGRATULATIONS! Immediately under it another one read: AND A SPECIAL WELCOME TO KALAWAKA—OUR VISITOR FROM DOWN UNDER!

Kalawaka looked up at Brad, who was looking down at him. Both started to laugh.

What a party! The room was crammed full of all kinds of people waiting to congratulate the guest of honor. There were people from all over Texas. There was a congressman and a senator there, and the governor of Texas sent his regrets. Kalawaka stayed close to Brad at first while Brad introduced him to the guests. He got along especially well with Luis Hernandez, the foreman. He swapped tales with some of the ranch hands, trying to top their stories of the modern "Wild West" with his own of the Outback.

At one point in the evening, Kalawaka heard an older gentleman say to Brad, "Well, Brad, it certainly is a lovely party."

"Thank you, Mr. Simmons. It certainly is."

"Just a shame those . . . uh . . . that kind got smuggled in here tonight." He motioned toward the group of employees.

Kalawaka watched as Brad straightened up, squared his shoulders, and furrowed his brow.

"No one was 'smuggled in' here tonight, Mr. Simmons. Mr. Hernandez happens to be one of my father's dear friends, as well as an excellent ranch manager. Mrs. Sanchez is virtually Todd's and my second mother. When our mother was ill years ago, she practically adopted us. Roberto Cruz and I played football together in high school, and he is one of my closest friends."

Mr. Simmons grew pale as Brad spoke. "Shucks, Brad, I really meant no harm. But you're right. I'm in no place to be criticizing your family's guest list. Uh, have a good evening and—congratulations." After an awkward moment, he nodded to Kalawaka and quickly disappeared in the crowd.

Tired from his long day and rather overwhelmed by the party, Kalawaka wandered down the hall away from

44

the hubbub. He found a large room lined with bookcases and filled with scattered couches and overstuffed chairs. Wearily, Kalawaka clambered up into a high-backed chair in one corner and settled back. The library was cool and quiet. A few lamps lit the room. When Mr. Collins and Brad's younger brother Todd entered and stood by the doorway, they never saw Kalawaka tucked away in the chair.

Neither of the men sat down. Mr. Collins leaned against the huge wooden desk and Todd leaned against a sofa. They were talking as they walked in, and Todd continued the conversation: "Dad, I feel like a failure. Like I'm not matching up to your expectations. This party for Brad really brings home to me what a failure I am."

There was silence for a moment and then Mr. Collins spoke, " 'Failure?' I'm not sure I understand, Son."

"My brother is only a year older than me, but he's gone to a big university and made it almost to the top of his class. He's a great football player. He's . . . he's a success at everything he does. I don't play football—I don't even like sports. I messed up the courses I tried to take here at the community college. Now Brad's been offered great jobs in both Houston and Dallas."

"Son, I wish you could see yourself as your mother and I see you. You are a kind person and always have been. You work hard, and you are indispensable to this ranch. Of course you and Brad are different. I'm glad you are. I wouldn't have it any other way. You do your best at being who you are. Brad is doing his best at being who he is. Your mom and I love you for who you are. And more than that, we respect you. And so does Brad. Granted, if you were to play football, you might look pretty silly. But I tell you, it's Brad who would look silly if he tried to run this place when we go on vacation. Mr. Hernandez tells me I can leave this entire operation in your hands and all will be well. You're my son and I'm very proud of you and your accomplishments. And I'm very proud of Brad's. But the thing I'm most proud of is who you both are."

"Do you really mean that, Dad?"

"Yes. Maybe I've never said it clearly enough before. But it's true."

"Thanks, Dad," Todd said quietly. "You're the greatest."

"You're the greatest, too, Son. Let's get back to the party." With that, they both left the room.

Kalawaka had contemplated trying to leave when they first entered, but they had blocked the doorway. In a way, he was glad he had stayed and overheard the conversation. He knew that a valuable lesson in caring had been played out right in front of him, but he wanted to check out exactly what it was with Sophie. She seemed to have the answer ready for him:

It's simple, Kalawaka. The members of the Collins family are accepting. They recognize the dignity of people, prize their worth, and respect their varied abilities and cultural backgrounds. It's the insides of others that is important to them, not the outsides. That kind of attitude is required for quality caring, too. There is no place for disregarding or mistreating others because they aren't carbon copies of you. Maybe they have different life-styles, or perhaps they do poorly what you do well. That's okay. Accept them and show it. Look how Brad stood up for his friends. Remember how Mr. Collins accepted Todd. And look how the Collins family accepted you—an unexpected guest and a foreign koala.

"Not to mention their acceptance of a certain know-it-all computer, my wise friend." Kalawaka laughed and returned to the party.

Humility like darkness, reveals the
heavenly lights.
—Henry David Thoreau

9

Unpretentious

THERE WAS A LIGHT RAIN after the party that night, but
the next morning dawned all the more fresh and clean
because of it. Just as the first rays of the sun fell on
Kalawaka's face, gently awakening him, he heard a soft
knock.

"Kalawaka, are you awake?" Brad whispered.

"Yes, I am, Brad. Come on in."

"I wondered if you would care to tour the ranch before
breakfast. It's beautiful at this time of the day."

"That sounds great!"

"Good! Be down at the stables as soon as you can."

"Stables!" Kalawaka said to himself. "Oh dear. What
have I gotten myself into?"

When Kalawaka arrived at the stables, Brad had already saddled up a chestnut gelding named Rake. "Good morning again, Kalawaka. The only real way to make the rounds is on horseback, of course." Brad mounted and then reached down for Kalawaka. Soon they were off.

Brad was right. The ranch was beautiful. As they rode along, Kalawaka said, "Brad, do you know how fortunate you are? You have a good head on your shoulders— I mean, I heard someone say last night that you graduated second in your class. You are an athlete. You have a great family, and you're a pretty nice guy to boot. You live here on this beautiful ranch, surrounded by everything you could possibly want. Most well-to-do humans I've met would let all that go to their head. But not you. You befriend a koala on a plane—and a perfect stranger of a koala at that—and then you bring him home. Your good friend Roberto is considered by at least one of your guests to be beneath you. It is kind of like you"— Kalawaka paused, groping for words, then rushed on— "value others as you value yourself." Kalawaka gasped, running out of breath at last.

Brad laughed. "Kalawaka, I am fortunate. I don't deny it. But you hit the nail on the head when you said 'value others.' I think that is an important key to enjoying life. Each person I meet is important, unique—unmapped territory just waiting to be explored. Take you, for instance. You have taught me so much about caring in this short time. I guess I've learned that there is always something I can learn from others. Everyone is unique and priceless!"

Kalawaka nodded and recalled Sophie's word *gift*. They were now on a bluff at the far end of the valley. The ranch was slowly coming to life before them on that glorious, sun-drenched morning. As they rode home, Kalawaka looked forward to getting back to hear Sophie's views on these matters before breakfast. And he did.

"Sophie, I've got something to say," he typed.

Ready.

"I'm not sure how to say this. When I started this journey to learn about quality caring, I had a couple of reasons. Of course, the first is that I wanted to learn more about caring, and caring is wonderful. But to be honest, the other reason I wanted to learn more about caring was to know something the other koalas in the grove didn't. I guess I wanted to impress them. Now that I've met Brad, I'm not so sure that was a good reason."

You're right, Kalawaka. When you're doing quality caring, you don't need to work to impress others. Being your best caring self allows others to see your good qualities naturally.

"I see, Sophie. Brad is like that. He has everything he could possibly want, but he doesn't show off. He simply is. And he still learns from others. Even me."

Brad is a very fortunate young man and a caring one. He's learned along the way to enjoy what others give of themselves to him—a big part of being unpretentious. On the one hand, Brad feels good about himself and knows he has something to give. On the other hand, he realizes that he doesn't know everything, and he doesn't pretend to, either. He has the humility and self-confidence to learn from others.

"I learned a lot about caring today, Sophie. It was a rather humbling experience, to say the least."

"There! You've got it!"

Never throughout history has a
man who lived a life of ease left a
name worth remembering.
—Theodore Roosevelt

10
Selfless

IT WAS WITH GREAT ANTICIPATION that Kalawaka arrived
in Los Angeles. Being, after all, a comparatively well-
educated koala, he knew no small amount of geography.
The ocean over which the sun sets in Los Angeles is the
same ocean over which the sun rises in Australia. He
longed to experience again the Pacific ocean—his ocean.

But it was night when he arrived; the ocean would
have to wait until morning. Because there was a marked
scarcity of trees, Kalawaka had just about resigned himself to sleeping in a bed again. But as he entered a nearby
hotel, fortunately he discovered a number of trees growing in the lobby: little islands of greenery amid a sea of
shining tile, glittering copper, and flashing chrome.

"A perfect tree!" Kalawaka squealed with delight. He
quickly climbed the tree and was asleep within minutes.

The sounds of breakfast in the hotel's restaurant awakened Kalawaka. The smell was tempting, but the lure of the ocean exerted a stronger pull. It was very early morning, but he managed to get a taxi to take him to the wharf. As he marveled at the sunlight dancing on the waves, soaked in the squawking of the gulls, and felt the salt breeze ruffle his fur, he was suddenly filled with an aching desire to be out there on the water.

A sport-fishing boat was scheduled to pull out in less than 20 minutes. Kalawaka hurriedly purchased a half-price ticket as a nonfisher, and climbed aboard, joining a wide array of people: middle-aged individuals with business worries still creasing their brows, older retired people whose faces shone like those of children on their birthdays, and young people with blaring radios and odd hairdos (even for humans). All in all, they were a cross section of the city that grew ever smaller as the boat headed out to sea. It would be a full hour before they arrived at the designated fishing spot, so Kalawaka sprawled in a deck chair, determined to enjoy every minute of the day and every inch of the experience.

Before long, a family of four attracted his attention. They were seated on a blanket eating their breakfast. The mother and father had bagels with cream cheese and their two girls had some sort of children's cereal.

But the older daughter—she may have been 11—protested: "Daddy, can't I have a bagel?"

"But honey, that is your favorite cereal."

"I know, but since we're all grown up and going fishing today, I want a bagel."

The younger daughter piped in: "Me too, Mommy and Daddy. Me too!" Exchanging looks of amused tolerance, the parents gave the kids the bagels in exchange for their cereal.

"Hmmm," Kalawaka said quietly to himself, "that was a kind thing for the parents to do. I wonder if that's part of what quality caring is all about—giving in to others." But only a few minutes later, Kalawaka saw that his hypothesis was only part of the story.

After breakfast, the father took out a pad and pencil and said to his wife, "Honey, would you mind keeping an eye on the kids so I can finish my report for work? It's due tomorrow morning."

"Of course not. Go ahead."

The father had been working for a few minutes when his younger daughter came up to him and said: "Daddy, can I please have a pencil and paper so I can draw?"

"No, honey. I can't give you any. I need to finish this report and this is the only paper and pencil I brought along."

Kalawaka puzzled for awhile. The matter wasn't as simple as it first appeared. The father wasn't giving in now. Something else was at work here that Kalawaka couldn't quite put his finger on. He felt sure that all he needed to do was to keep his eye on that family to find out what was going on. Something about that family was very "right."

The captain's voice came over the loudspeaker, announcing that people could start fishing. To Kalawaka's surprise, the father didn't fish at all! He spent all his time fixing the girls' rods and helping them to fish. The fellow obviously knew a great deal about fishing, and he passed it on to the girls as he helped them. The mother, it was apparent, wasn't along to fish. She encouraged the girls, but she didn't seem particularly excited at the prospect of baiting a hook.

For three hours that father helped those little girls fish. They even managed to catch a few small ones. And the man was content to do what he was doing. No, more than content, he was so immersed in the girls' pleasure that Kalawaka was willing to bet he never even thought about what he was missing.

Kalawaka was thoroughly relishing this day on his ocean. Everyone on the boat who wanted to catch some fish had, except for two men fishing side by side. One was retired and the other was a middle-aged business-man on vacation from Denver. As the day wore on these men became increasingly frustrated with the prospect of returning to port empty-handed. The captain had just finished announcing that the boat would be heading back in half an hour when he excitedly shouted, "Folks, there's a school of bonita swimming straight toward us. Get ready to catch some fish!"

"Ah," Kalawaka said to himself happily, "those two men will have a chance to catch some fish after all." As the school swam toward the boat, people began pulling in fish right and left. The two men, greatly relieved, felt tugs on their lines. They were both excitedly playing their fish and reeling them in when they realized there was a problem. The lines weren't going anywhere. From above, the captain shouted, "Your lines are tangled to-gether. One of you is going to have to cut your line."

Kalawaka saw a pained look cross both men's faces, and then they turned back in a last, determined attempt to prevent that unhappy occurrence. When it was ap-parent that the captain was right, the businessman pulled a penknife out of his pocket and quietly cut his line.

"I say!" Kalawaka mumbled under his breath.

Sunset that day found Kalawaka on the beach watch-ing the sun sink behind his ocean. He fed the experiences of the day into Sophie, who told him:

Quality caring is selfless. Acting selflessly means consciously setting aside your own needs in order to meet the needs of another. That is not the same as ignoring your own needs or allowing others to walk all over you, nor does it mean that you always give others what they want. You watched the mother and father give up their bagel, but the father kept his pad and pencil. The businessman made a conscious choice to cut his line and give pleasure to another.

When you do quality caring, you actively choose to meet the needs of others rather than using others to meet your needs. In that way, you care for others with no strings attached.

"Thanks, Sophie. I've learned a lot and you've taught me a lot. I'd like to see a summary of everything I've learned so far."

Okay, that's an easy one. Here it is. Quality caring is:
- GENUINE
- EMPATHIC
- PATIENT
- AVAILABLE
- PRESENT
- CONFRONTIVE
- DEPENDABLE
- ACCEPTING
- UNPRETENTIOUS
- SELFLESS

As Kalawaka read the list Sophie displayed, it was like reading a roll-call of the examples of caring he had encountered so far on his quest. As he watched the sun disappear into the ocean off the California coast, he felt alone and a little homesick. "It would be easy to catch a plane from here to home," he said to himself. "Yes, I'll do just that! What more is there for me to learn about quality caring, anyway?"

But at the airport, something happened that opened Kalawaka's eyes to see how much more there was to learn about quality caring than he had thought. He soon realized that he had not even reached the halfway point in his quest.

Here ends Part One of *The Quest for Quality Caring*. Part Two is called "What Quality Caring Is Not." It chronicles the many discoveries that disclosed to Kala-waka exactly what quality caring *isn't*.

Part Two

What Quality Caring Is Not

They are playing a game. They are
playing at not playing a game. If I
show them I see they are, I shall break
the rules and they will punish me. I
must play their game, of not seeing I
see the game.

—R. D. Laing

1

Game Playing

THE LOS ANGELES AIRPORT was a veritable beehive of
activity—airline workers, service personnel, and trav-
elers jostling one another, heading to their own desti-
nations. Kalawaka had experienced some busy airports
before, but the explosion of energy he witnessed here
was something new. Exhausted from his attempt to cross
the main terminal and pick up a ticket (he had to dodge
the careless feet of countless people too busy to notice
a koala beneath them), he spied a newly vacated seat,
cautiously ran over, and plopped down.

"Ah," he said to himself, "it will be so nice to get away
from all this incessant movement and be home in my
quiet grove again."

After catching his breath, Kalawaka pulled out some
eucalyptus leaves for a munch. As he stuffed a whole

handful in his mouth, the people around him all got up and left.

Oh my, he thought, *I hope they weren't offended that I didn't offer them any leaves.* But then he surmised that their flight had been announced. He wasn't alone for long, though. Many people came along to replace the ones who had left. He first noticed a young couple talking excitedly with a man:

"Just imagine, Europe!"

"I don't understand why you are so excited," the man replied.

"We're going to London, Paris, Rome—all the great cities."

"Oh, this must be your first trip to Europe." Yawning conspicuously, he added, "I suppose I was somewhat excited my first time. Let me see . . . this will be my third trip to Europe—this year," he replied, looking utterly bored.

Kalawaka was unnerved by this, but he didn't know why. Something made him feel uncomfortable. He listened some more.

"So, you're stopping in Paris?" the man asked the couple.

"Oh, yes," the woman answered. "The city of lights."

"*Il faût que vous passez du temps au Louvre,*" the man began, but stopped when he saw the puzzled looks on their faces. Apparently pained, he continued: "Oh, I'm so sorry. You don't speak French. I was just saying that you simply *must* spend some time at the Louvre."

"Well . . . ah . . . yes, we'd planned to," the woman answered, a bit embarrassed.

Kalawaka knew that something uncaring was going on, but before he had a chance to plug the data into Sophie, another conversation attracted his attention. A man was just returning to his seat, and a woman spoke to him.

"Did you call her, dear?"

"No."

"No? But why not? She wanted you to telephone before we left for the weekend."

"Well, I decided not to. We asked Megan to come home early last night. I could have talked to her then, but she didn't care about what we wanted. So, I'm not going to call her now."

"Okay, dear," the woman said quietly, "but you know she wanted to talk to you."

"That'll just teach her a lesson," he replied.

Now Kalawaka's fur was bristling. It was almost like— yes! These people were playing games. Not the nice, cute, harmless games young koalas learn to play, but hurtful games.

The revelation struck Kalawaka like a cricket bat on the head. "I know what quality caring is, true enough, but I haven't learned a thing about what it isn't—until now. I can't go home yet. There's too much left to learn." In that moment, Kalawaka decided to continue his quest, backtracking through the U.S.A. and Europe to find out what quality caring *isn't*. As he resolved to do just that, a third conversation broke his concentration.

"No, dear, I wouldn't dream of flying coach." She shuddered delicately, as though the idea of flying coach was akin to contracting the plague. "Heavens, I'm all over the Continent—you know, Paris, Geneva, Vienna— well, my dear, you know I must have my comforts. I'm sure you understand."

Kalawaka felt sick to his stomach.

"Darling, that's why I always take the Concorde whenever I fly."

"Good grief," Kalawaka muttered, picking up Sophie and walking away.

Outside, he hailed a cab and headed to the nearest bus station.

> People show their character in nothing
> more clearly than by what they think
> laughable.
> —Johann Wolfgang von Goethe

2

Sarcastic

THE LONG BUS RIDE across the arid Nevada countryside left Kalawaka with quite a thirst. He had already learned that it was a rarity in this country to find a freshwater spring outdoors where thirsty koalas could find a cool drink. No, here people always went inside for that. Well, he knew he wasn't the only thirsty passenger on the bus. He trailed along behind a group of fellow riders until they entered an establishment called "The Long Branch Inn." Being a koala, he knew all about branches.

As his eyes grew accustomed to the dim light, he realized that this was not what he had expected at all. The place certainly did not have any branches. Plenty of stools and chairs and tables—but not one branch. He got over his initial disappointment and ordered a glass of water. The waiter scowled and set the water down hard, saying, "Here you go, big spender!" Kalawaka wondered how much water cost. As he was sipping, he looked around. People were having a good time, but one table in particular drew his attention. These folks were laughing so loud they almost seemed to be howling.

They seem happy, he thought. *A lot of quality caring must be going on. I probably won't find out much about what quality caring isn't around here.* Kalawaka headed for a nearby table. A smartly dressed woman and three men in business suits sat at another table, smiling and laughing over their meal. As he took his seat near their table, he heard one of them say to another, "Look, Curly, you should give our lady vice president some respect." A round of deep, throaty laughter broke out.

The name *Curly* instantly caught Kalawaka's attention. He knew a great deal about curls, being the furry creature he was. As their conversation continued, however, Kalawaka was quite shocked to learn that Curly was the tall man without any hair.

Kalawaka set his glass down and scratched his head, a little confused. Something was not right here, but he couldn't put his finger on it. Just then a voice from another table interrupted his train of thought.

"Hey, Speedy, how about some service here?" The man was talking to the waiter—a nervous young fellow, obviously new on the job. There was no doubt that the poor chap was slow, very slow, and to top it off he was having a terrible time remembering which orders went to which table.

Kalawaka exclaimed to himself, "Why do these people use words that don't seem to fit?" They call a bald man 'Curly' and a slow waiter 'Speedy.' I'm perplexed!"

"*Sure*, Mary—uh—I mean Ms. Vice President. We all know the only reason you got your position was because you're so good at your job." They all laughed again. "The idea of quotas just never entered our heads," another man snorted. Mary, still laughing, excused herself and left.

"What are they smiling about?" wondered Kalawaka. "Their voices aren't happy. Their words don't make me feel warm and friendly. Why, look how tense they all are." Kalawaka began to wonder if smiles and laughter always do point to caring or happiness.

The stuffiness and the loud music inside the Long Branch Inn were too much for him, so he picked up Sophie and went outside. Kalawaka offered Sophie a description of all he had experienced, and she replied:

> What you saw inside is called sarcasm. Sarcasm involves saying the exact opposite of what you mean in such a way that the other person understands your put-down. Interestingly enough, the word comes from Greek and means "flesh tearing." In common usage, it means any verbal exchange that depreciates the dignity and value of another.

"Sophie, that's terrible! How uncaring! Why would anyone engage in such behavior?"

> Many times open sarcasm discloses a person who is uncomfortable with himself or herself and belies this with ridiculing behavior.

"How sad!" Kalawaka sighed. "Those people inside seem to be missing so much of what relationships are all about. So, sarcastic is another thing that quality caring isn't."

They surfeited with honey and began
to loathe the taste of sweetness,
whereof a little more than a little is by
much too much.

—Shakespeare

3

Artificially Sweet

A RATHER PUZZLING INCIDENT took place the day Ka-lawaka arrived in Philadelphia. He knew that the name means "City of Brotherly Love," and frankly he didn't anticipate learning much about what caring isn't. Setting work aside for the moment, he decided to enjoy touring the city. First he went to a tourist information center.

It was 4:55 P.M. when Kalawaka opened the door of the information center, jingling a bell. Now koalas have an acute sense of hearing, so Kalawaka heard a woman in the back saying, "Oh, no! Why do they always have to come here right before we close? These people make me so mad!" A moment later a woman appeared through a door behind the counter, all smiles, and in a sweet voice she almost sang, "Why, helloooo! Welcome to Phil-adelphia. Can I help you?" Kalawaka couldn't believe his ears. Could this sweet voice be the same one he had heard just a moment ago? The sudden shift was almost enough to make him forget what he came for in the first place.

"Huh?—Oh, yes. I just arrived in town—I'm from Australia, you see—and I'd like some information about Philadelphia."

Again she almost sang, "My pleasure! I'll be glad to get you *everything* you need." At that moment, a man hollered from the back. "June, are you ready to go?"

"In a minute, Jack," she sang. "We have a little visitor here from Australia who needs our help. We'll do *all* we can to take care of him." She smiled at Kalawaka. "Now, you stay right there. I'll be right back with *everything* you need, dear."

"Maybe she wasn't the one I heard," Kalawaka said to himself. "She seems so nice."

So Kalawaka was astounded to hear the woman speaking in the back room, no mistaking her this time. "There's some disgusting, flea-bitten creature out there wanting information about Philadelphia. Why do these foreign types always have to walk in here right at the end of the day? They sure have their nerve."

The next moment she walked back out and handed Kalawaka his material. Smiling a smile that never reached her eyes, almost oozing sweetness, she said, "Here you are. Now if there is *anything* else we can do for you while you're here, you just let us know. It's our pleasure."

Kalawaka stared at her askance, grabbed his materials with a quick "Thanks," and scurried out. He turned to Sophie and asked, "What on earth was going on in there?"

Kalawaka, you could call that woman artificially sweet. A six-dollar word for the same thing is *cloying*, which means "so sweet as to be disgusting or distasteful, excessively sweet or sentimental."

Her too-sweet manner of relating hides a great deal of stored-up hostility. On the surface, it might seem that her disguising of her negative feelings is kind and considerate, but, in fact, the opposite is true. The constant gushiness prevents her from dealing constructively with her anger and robs others of the opportunity to relate to her realistically and honestly. Quality caring means not hiding your feelings under sticky-sweet words and actions.

"Do you mean she should have said all those insulting remarks to my face? I wouldn't have liked that, either."

Sophie pondered, which for her necessitated whir-rings and clicks while she searched her data banks.

No. But this goes back to being genuine, which is one of those things quality caring is. She could have said, "I'm sorry if I seem abrupt. I was just about to close up when you arrived." That way she would have been clear and honest in the messages she was sending you while acknowledging that it was her problem, not yours.

"You know, Soph, when I was around her I felt sticky—like she was pouring syrup all over me. Even if I hadn't overheard her talking in the back, I think I would have known something was amiss. She was so sicken-ingly sweet, I felt like I needed a bath!"

Oh, the wasted hours of life
That have drifted by!
Oh, the good that might have been,
Lost without a sigh!
—Sarah Doudney

4

Being Swept Along

Many sights in Philadelphia fascinated Kalawaka, but none as much as a side trip he took to Mount Holly, New Jersey, to visit the Relief Fire Company, one of the oldest operating volunteer fire departments in the United States. It was there that a most unlikely thing happened. He was touring the station and became so absorbed by the shiny red truck and the complex apparatus on it that he climbed up to get a better look. No sooner had he done so than the screech of a siren split the air and people began running and shouting.

"Oh no! What did I do now?" Kalawaka wailed. But in the sudden explosion of activity, no one seemed to notice him. People came running from all over. They ran to put on special coats and boots that lined the wall, and then, with a roar, the truck he was sitting on took off.

It was the fastest, noisiest ride Kalawaka had ever taken. The truck cut around corners at high speed, and from every direction cars and people made way for it. Just as Kalawaka was beginning to enjoy the ride, they screeched to a halt right in front of a modest home set back from the road. A man ran toward them across the lawn, shouting, "Please save my house!"

Kalawaka spotted an army of flames licking their way around a closed window on the second floor. The glass clouded and cracked from the heat. The magnitude of the task before the volunteer fire fighters awed Kalawaka, but they were more than equal to the job.

As the captain barked out orders, the fire fighters forced the flames to retreat, pace by pace. It was a grueling assault, but within an hour the battle was won, and only isolated pockets of resistance remained for the volunteers. During the fray, Kalawaka was intrigued by one fellow who seemed to be everywhere. It appeared that he did enough for two men. This was only natural because, as it turned out, "he" *was* two men: identical twins. When Kalawaka first saw the two side by side, he was astonished. He had heard of koala twins, but they were quite rare. Yet here before him stood identical human twins—and caring ones at that. Wasn't it caring to put out fires, saving lives and property?

Right away he made up his mind to have a word with the two after they were finished with their work. "What a marvelous opportunity!" he exclaimed. "Caring twins." So when they walked toward the truck and sat down in the grass beside it, Kalawaka shouted down from the truck, "Excuse me. Would it be possible to have a word with you two? You see, I'm from Australia and doing some research on caring." The two men, amazed, looked up at the truck. They could scarcely believe their eyes. "Hey, Stephen! Do you see what I see?"

"I do, Stuart, if what you see is a koala bear."

They started firing questions at Kalawaka, starting with what he was doing on the fire truck in the first place, and going on to ask about the nature of his research. After taking some pains to explain that he was a marsupial and most definitely not a bear, Kalawaka described his quest, and the men agreed to answer a few questions. But Kalawaka's first question was interrupted by another fire fighter shouting, "Stephen, could you give me a hand over here for a minute?"

"Sure thing!" Stephen shouted, and then said to Kalawaka, "I'll be back later."

Kalawaka sensed how uneasy Stuart was. "I really ought to be over there helping, but I guess you need to talk to me, too. What kind of questions did you have in mind?"

"Well, Stuart, I want to know why you are a volunteer fire fighter."

He thought for a moment. "That's simple. I do it because I should do it. Somebody asked me to be a volunteer fire fighter, and I just couldn't say no."

"How do you like doing this?"

Stuart furrowed his brow and said, "Like it? Well, I guess I never thought about it. It's not really something you like; it's just something you do."

"Do you do other caring for people besides this?"

"Well, I sing in a barbershop quartet at a rest home on the third Tuesday of every month. You know, whenever there's a need, I feel like a strong river current is pulling me along. When someone asks me, I just can't say no. It's something I just have to do."

"Stuart, how would you complete this sentence? Caring is_____."

Stuart thought for a moment and then said with a sigh: "Caring is my duty."

Just as Stuart completed that sentence, Stephen came back. "Stuart, they need you over there." He excused himself and left.

"Now, Mr. Kalawaka, what can I do for you?"

"Stephen, I'll start with the same questions I asked Stuart. Why do you care for people and help them?"

"You mean fire fighting?"

Kalawaka nodded.

"I care because I care. I enjoy helping others, and I know how very important fire fighting is."

"Are you involved in other kinds of caring?"

"I guess so. I'm an assistant Boy Scout leader."

"Why do you do that?"

"It's enjoyable—and I love kids." Stephen paused and looked at Kalawaka. "Not when they act up, mind you, but I do enjoy them in the long run. This is something good I can do for the kids and my community—a little shaping of tomorrow's adults, I guess."

"You're different from Stuart," Kalawaka observed.

"I imagine that's true in some ways. Stuart sometimes worries me in a lot of the things he ends up doing. He gets involved in things without giving them much thought. And you know something? Sometimes when he gets swept along like that, I think he ends up disliking what he's doing. I guess he has just never learned to say "no" and people take advantage of him. Of course, there are times I wonder what I got myself into. Like when the siren goes off at 2:30 A.M. and I'm in bed, or on days when the Scouts and I seem to have different ideas about what we're doing. But a long time ago I made a decision about what I wanted to do. That decision—and knowing that in the end I enjoy it—keeps me going even in those doubtful moments. You know, the ones that come in the middle of the night."

"Stephen," Kalawaka asked, "How would you complete this sentence? 'Caring is_____.' "

"Hmmm! I guess I'd say caring is . . . satisfying and sometimes enjoyable hard work."

"Thanks, Stephen, for talking with me."

As the fire truck pulled away, Kalawaka turned to Sophie. "Well, that was interesting. I think I see what quality caring isn't, but I don't know exactly how to put it."

Stephen said it well when he described his brother as "swept along." Stuart allows people and circumstances to influence him too much. By forgetting his own needs, desires, and feelings, he unwittingly allows himself to be "caught in the flow"— with unfortunate results. He ends up feeling trapped into doing things he doesn't like or really want to do, losing himself in the process and feeling angry and resentful.

On the other hand, Stephen is intentional about what he does. He considers his needs, desires, and feelings before he gets involved in caring. Because he is aware of his own needs, Stephen feels free to say yes or no to each opportunity to care. He carefully selects ways to care, choosing things he enjoys and wants to do. This keeps him going even when caring becomes hard work.

"Thanks, Sophie," Kalawaka said and suddenly grimaced. "Oh, no! I just realized how I got here. Now I'm going to have to walk back to town."

Let's get going, then.

Suffering, and nothing else, will
implant that sentiment of
responsibility which is the
first step to reform.

—James Bryce

5

Rescuing

ANOTHER WEEK PASSED, and Kalawaka decided it was
time to head back to Europe. Portugal was one country
he had hoped to visit earlier, but the opportunity had
not presented itself. Now was the time. So he booked
a flight to Lisbon.

A seasoned world traveler now, Kalawaka found taxi
rides, hotel reservations, and accommodations almost
routine. Arrival in Lisbon went without a hitch. After a
day of busy sight-seeing in the heart of Lisbon, Kalawaka
headed for a drinking establishment. Koalas enjoy a
drink almost as much as they enjoy a munch on eucalyptus leaves. Not alcohol, mind you, but water, tea, or
coffee.

As he sipped from a tall glass of iced coffee, a stout
gentleman with graying hair stumbled onto the stool

beside him. *Oh, dear!* thought Kalawaka as the stench of alcohol engulfed him. *This fellow's been tipping the bottle a bit too much.* Before long, Kalawaka's neighbor passed out right on the serving counter and slid to the floor.

"Joaquim!" a voice bellowed from the entrance. "What do you think you're doing? Call the police to get that drunk out of here." "Oh, Señor Pereira, please let's not call the police. I know him. Let me call his family and they will come to get him. They always do."

The owner frowned at the bartender. "Oh, all right, Joaquim. But the next time he comes in here drunk, you are to call the police immediately."

Joaquim used the phone located right on the counter where Kalawaka was seated. With his keen sense of hearing, he overheard both ends of the telephone conversation.

"Señora Lopes?"

"Yes."

"This is Joaquim da Silva, the bartender at Port Lisbon."

"No! Not again."

"I'm afraid so, Señora Lopes. Could you come here right away?"

"My son isn't home. I don't know how I could manage alone."

"You must. Quickly. My boss, he's even threatened to call the police."

"No! No police. I'll be there as fast as I can."

Within a quarter of an hour, Señora Lopes stepped through the door. Her husband, still out cold, lay under a barstool. After an unsuccessful attempt to move him alone, she cast a pleading glance at the bartender. Joaquim came around to help her get her husband out of the bar and into the car. Even he was having difficulty, so Kalawaka quickly finished his drink and lent a hand—or paw. Loading Señor Lopes into the car convinced Kalawaka that Señora Lopes still had an impossible task before her.

"Ma'am, I would be happy to ride along and help you get him into your home."

Relief flooded her worried face. "I'd appreciate that so much. You certainly are very kind, not to mention strong."

Strength was exactly what Kalawaka needed to pull, push, and shove Señor Lopes from the car to his bedroom. But amidst much groaning and straining the two of them managed to get it done.

"Señor Kalawaka, I don't know how to thank you. At least you must stay here this evening as our guest. Yes?"

"Why thank you so much, Señora Lopes. If you don't mind, I did notice a most exceptional tree growing in front of your home—I much prefer trees to beds—perhaps I could lodge there?"

"Certainly!" she exclaimed.

Kalawaka was exhausted. Sight-seeing in Lisbon was tiring enough, but the ordeal with Señor Lopes had completely done him in. No sooner had he climbed the tree than he was sound asleep.

A telephone conversation from an upstairs bedroom awakened Kalawaka the next morning. From his branch right beside the window, he heard Señora Lopes speaking.

"Hello, Señor Bargas. This is Helena Lopes."

"Where is he? It's late and he has a meeting."

"Oh, I'm sorry. He's sick with the flu."

"The flu? Again?"

"Yes, I'm sure he'll be better tomorrow."

Kalawaka felt very very sad. "Señora Lopes seems to care very much about her husband, but something is not quite right here," he mused to himself. The elements of caring did seem to be there, like the pieces of a puzzle. Yet when the pieces were put together, the result was not at all satisfying. "Maybe you can tell me about this, Soph. I don't understand. Señora Lopes's actions looked like caring, but I suspect they weren't caring at all."

I couldn't have said it better myself, Kalawaka. When you continually bail others out of problem situations—situations that they have brought upon themselves—you take away their responsibility. If they lose this sense of responsibility, they will never change or grow. Taking responsibility away from someone is called *rescuing*, and it signals that quality caring is not happening—even if on the surface it looks like caring. Rescuing behavior is subtle. It almost seems as if you are doing the other person a favor. Not so. It is often hard to do what outwardly looks uncaring—for example, allowing Señor Lopes to spend the night in jail. Having to take responsibility for himself may hurt for the present, but it has great long-term healing potential. Rescuing is not quality caring.

You love me so much, you want to
put me in your pocket. And I
should die there smothered.
—D. H. Lawrence

6

Possessive

THE ROAD FROM CORDOBA to Seville was long, dusty,
and lonely. Kalawaka progressed at a reasonably quick
pace for a koala carrying a computer. He had heard many
good things about El Mercado de Seville, and he was
anxious to get there. As he hurried along, he caught
sight of two women on the road who evidently were
heading for the same market. In any case, they were
carrying large, empty baskets.

Coming close to them, Kalawaka was considering
whether to ask if he could walk with them when he
realized the two were deep in conversation. One of the
women said, "Pilar, I would like to tell you a story. Once
there was a lady who was very bighearted. She always

cared for people and animals who came her way. One day when she was walking in her garden, she came upon a little bird with a broken wing. She quickly stooped down and gathered the trembling bird in her hands, took it inside, and set about fixing its wing. It took weeks for the little bird's wing to mend, and during that time the kind lady kept the bird in a cage. She came to love the little bird greatly, and the bird returned her affection.

"But the day came when the little bird's wing was healed, and the lady began to feel sad. She wanted to keep the bird, but she knew that the bird would grow unhappy in the cage. Her great heart almost burst. She took the little bird out of its cage, walked outside, and with tears in her eyes, set it free. The bird chirped for joy and flew high and far. When it was out of sight, the woman, happy for the bird but distressed for herself, started to go back inside. Just before she opened the door, she heard a flutter. The little bird landed on her shoulder—chirping louder than ever. She understood that the bird was now free to give her the gift of friendship—as it could never have done from the cage."

"Oh, Rosa," Pilar exclaimed. "You're trying to tell me something."

"Perhaps I am."

"You know how I feel about my precious daughter Luisa. Luisa is like that little bird, isn't she?"

"Yes, she is."

"You understand, and you told me this story to help me see how foolish I've been." Pilar stopped and gave Rosa a big hug, saying, "You're a dear friend, Rosa!"

The scene astounded Kalawaka. As the women continued down the road, never even noticing him, he asked Sophie what had happened. She simply said:

"If you love something, set it free. If it returns to you, it's really yours. If it doesn't, it never was."

I don't like those cold, precise
perfect people who, in order not to
speak wrong, never speak at all, and
in order not to do wrong,
never do anything.
—Henry Ward Beecher

7

Disavowing of Authority

WHEN KALAWAKA RETURNED TO GERMANY he remembered the kindness of the Kaiser family and thought about dropping in to visit them once more. But he decided against it because he did not have enough time; his eucalyptus leaves were running low.

Before he left Australia, his third cousin, Kamchuka, had told him to be sure to visit at least one of the fine automobile factories in Europe. Kamchuka ran a small factory of his own for processing eucalyptus leaves into a variety of delectable delights, and he wanted to know how the factories "up-over" operated. Kalawaka, having worked a couple of summers for Kamchuka, was a mite curious himself. So, instead of heading south to Garmisch–Partenkirchen, he went north, to a factory that advertised guided tours.

There Kalawaka was made a most welcome guest. After touring the factory, the guide realized that the visitor from down under was interested in employee relationships as well as factory procedures, so he introduced Kalawaka to the plant personnel director.

"Frau Kleinfelder, this is Kalawaka. He is a visitor from Australia and is most interested in how so many people work together successfully. Perhaps you could have a chat."

"Surely. Won't you come into my office, Mr. Kalawaka?"

Frau Kleinfelder turned out to be helpful and most professional. She described the ins and outs of employee relationships at the plant and then added: "But do you know what I've discovered to be the most important key to supervisor-employee relationships?"

Kalawaka shook his head.

"It's the proper use of authority by the supervisors. Let me illustrate. We have one supervisor who utterly rejects the idea of being an authority figure to his department. He likes to say, 'We're all equals here.' Now, that's true enough in one sense. I mean, there are certain rights that every person possesses. But when those you are supposed to be supervising approach you with a serious problem, they aren't looking for a discourse on equality. They expect a decision from the supervisor that will help resolve the problem. Just the other day, two individuals in his department had a disagreement. True to form, he declined to interfere. Well, they 'solved' it on their own all right. Now they don't speak to each other at all. The tension in that department has been steadily increasing.

"Kalawaka," Frau Kleinfelder continued, "are you surprised to learn that that supervisor's department is the least productive department in the plant? His employees spend more time squabbling than working. Often his workers don't even have a clear idea of what they are supposed to be doing. Many times he says, 'We're all equals here. You decide what needs to be done next.' Without an overall plan in his department, it's no wonder that little is ever accomplished. We have agreed to let him continue in his supervisory capacity for a while, because we hope to teach him how to exercise his authority constructively."

"But isn't participatory decision making good?" asked Kalawaka, who had discussed this very issue with his cousin Kamchuka.

"In many instances," said Frau Kleinfelder. "Certainly a good supervisor will seek out suggestions and information from the employees. But sometimes there must be one person from whom a decision must come. Otherwise, endless frustration could result. And that is where this supervisor is not doing a supervisor's job."

Kalawaka left a little confused, so he turned to Sophie. She said:

> Kalawaka, proper use of authority is another important key to quality caring. Failure to use authority properly blocks good caring. Some people mistakenly believe that any use of authority destroys individual freedom. It is the misuse and nonuse of authority that does that. Properly used, authority allows individuals to exercise their freedom in a pleasant, well-ordered environment and protects their personal freedom as well. Proper use of authority is also an important part of good government, for example. Of course, authority can be misused, but it is important to remember that failure to use authority is as bad as the misuse of it. Proper use of rightful authority is most caring.

"I see," said Kalawaka. "So one who would be involved in quality caring doesn't disavow authority, but claims the authority that rightly belongs to him or her in the caring relationship. And that helps the care receiver to grow."

Very good, Kalawaka. You are getting to be almost as quick as a computer.

"Thanks for the compliment," said Kalawaka, "I think."

He had only one vanity;
he thought he could
give advice better than
any other person.
—Mark Twain

8

Problem Solving

Rome was a city Kalawaka truly enjoyed in all its magnificence—the statues, the fountains, the crumbling Colosseum. Kalawaka sat down on the steps of a courthouse dating from the days when Italy was united in the nineteenth century and watched the pigeons perform their awkward strut on the sidewalk. A few minutes later, two men came out of the courthouse and sat down behind him.

"Well, it's really over. I never thought it would end this way. I don't know what I'm going to do now—"

"Oh, you'll be all right. What makes you think it is going to be so terrible?"

"I guess I'm afraid of being alone. Going home to an empty apartment every day—"

"So you can buy a pet. A dog or cat. That's just what you need to keep you company. A pet will take the chill off an empty home."

"I guess, but a pet is hardly a substitute for a person."

"Yes, I know. That's why it would also help you to get involved in some new activities. How about joining the club I go to? You could meet plenty of people there who would make fine companions."

"It just seems too soon—"

"Soon? You need to get involved in things again. I'll pick you up at seven and we'll go tonight."

"Guiseppe, I do feel a little lost, but—"

"See! Aimless. You need to be thinking about this whole thing in a much more positive light. Divorce isn't the end of the world. I know no better cure for aimlessness than a good, full routine."

"A routine?"

"Exactly. Let's sit down and I'll help you work one out. How about tonight over dinner?"

"Well, no thanks, Guiseppe. I'd kind of like to be alone tonight."

"Nonsense. I thought you said you didn't want to be alone. Of course, if you want to be alone, the pet idea wouldn't be so good."

"You're right, I suppose. Look, Guiseppe, I need to go now."

"Sure. But—"

Kalawaka lost the rest of the conversation as the two disappeared into the crowd on the sidewalk. *Another lesson in what caring isn't*, he thought as he opened up Sophie and filled her in on what he had just witnessed. She replied:

Quality caring isn't problem solving or cranking out suggestions. Often another person's needs are far deeper than they may appear to you. Many feelings and thoughts—some of them the other person isn't even aware of—need to be dealt with. Guiseppe was trying to put a Band-Aid over his friend's gaping wound. What a mistake! Quality caring doesn't attempt to treat large wounds superficially, trying to give easy answers to difficult life situations. Life is too complicated for such pre-packaged solutions.

"Help me sort out three of these last four lessons, Sophie. I've learned that quality caring isn't rescuing, isn't disavowing of authority, and isn't problem solving. Somehow these seem related to me, and maybe a little contradictory."

Okay, let's take them one at a time, Kalawaka.

1. A rescuer is one who consistently bails another out of a jam—preventing the other from experiencing the consequences of his or her actions.
2. A disavower of authority is one who refuses to claim the authority that is rightfully his or hers to assert in a specific caring situation.
3. A problem solver is one who rushes in to offer advice and minor solutions to major difficulties.

This is why quality caring is hard work, Kalawaka. You must learn to choose wisely among many options in order to care most effectively.

"Thanks, Sophie. You aren't kidding, it's hard. In these situations, I guess people (and koalas) need to solve their own problems."

Right!

It had been a long and exciting quest, but Kalawaka was a little homesick. The bag of eucalyptus leaves his mother gave him was running dangerously low. He had learned so much about what caring is and what it isn't, and he was tired of just watching. He was itching to return home to do some caring of his own. So Kalawaka made his way to the airport in Rome and booked the next flight to Adelaide. As the plane took off, he gazed fondly at Sophie. "I wonder," Kalawaka mused, "if there will be as much to learn and do at home? By the way, Sophie, what have I learned so far?"

Coming right up. You've learned that quality caring isn't:
- GAME PLAYING
- SARCASTIC
- ARTIFICIALLY SWEET
- BEING SWEPT ALONG
- RESCUING
- POSSESSIVE
- DISAVOWING OF AUTHORITY
- PROBLEM SOLVING

As Kalawaka read the list, he remembered the examples of nonquality caring they represented. All lessons in how *not* to care. Kalawaka filed them away mentally, glad of his new learning.

Here ends Part Two of *The Quest for Quality Caring*. Part Three is entitled "Kalawaka's Guide to Quality Caring." It recounts the many discoveries Kalawaka made when he returned home to Australia and set about putting quality caring into action.

Part Three

Kalawaka's Guide to Quality Caring

God has given us two hands—
one to receive with and
the other to give with.
—Billy Graham

1

Receive Graciously

WHEN KALAWAKA ARRIVED HOME in mid-morning, he was dead tired. It had been a long journey to his grove from the Adelaide airport, and the time difference had his inside clock all confused. His mother was just putting away the breakfast leaves when Kalawaka climbed the tree.

"Kalawaka!" she exclaimed. "My boy! We're so happy you're back." She went on and on as mother koalas tend to do when their children return from being gone a long time.

Hearing the commotion, Kalawaka's father climbed down to the kitchen branch to see what was going on. When he saw his son, he was so happy he almost tumbled out of the tree. After welcoming him back and taking a good look at him he said, "Son, you look tired. It must be jet lag."

Kalawaka nodded in agreement. "I sure could use a nap." He climbed up to his old branch and looked around. He was pleased to see that it was exactly as he had left it. He was asleep in minutes.

When he awoke some hours later, he looked around and sighed, "Home at last. How wonderful!" Hearing him stir, his mother called, "Kalawaka, we have a surprise for you. Come on down."

"A surprise!" Kalawaka exclaimed. "I'll be right down."

Well, the surprise was a koala party in his honor— and if anyone knows how to throw a party, it's a group of koalas. Guests began arriving at seven. An hour later, Kalawaka looked around and thought, *Every koala in the grove must be here. There are some koalas here I haven't seen in years, and others I don't even think I know.*

All the koalas seemed interested in hearing about his quest, and Kalawaka was unabashed in his enjoyment of telling them stories about the places he had been and the sights he had seen. In a rather hushed moment after he finished relating the story about horseback riding on Brad's ranch one koala said, "Goodness sakes, Kalawaka, your venturing out into the world was a very brave thing to do."

Kalawaka smiled. "Thank you. At times, it was rather frightening, but it sure was exciting."

The chatter resumed and the evening passed at a leisurely pace. Kalawaka hadn't noticed at first that his Uncle Ed had not accompanied Aunt Mathilda to the party. No big surprise really. Uncle Ed never was too terribly fond of large gatherings, and since Aunt Mathilda seemed in a rather grouchy mood, Kalawaka was sure that they had argued about going. "Some things never change," he said to himself.

Just then his younger brother Kawana came up to him and asked to see him alone. They climbed to a more private branch and Kawana handed a small package to Kalawaka. "It's a gift for you, Kalawaka."

Kalawaka untied the string and opened the package. Inside were some very expensive eucalyptus tea leaves, a special blend that was Kalawaka's favorite. He blinked back a tear or two and gave his brother a hug. "Thank you, Kawana." Kawana smiled.

After a brotherly chat, Kawana said, "Maybe we should go back to the party now."

As Kalawaka dressed for bed that night, he thought about the day and felt good, very good. His wonderful welcome, the homecoming party, the compliments he had received, and the special gift from Kawana all filled him with joy. "It was a marvelous day. And being genuine, being myself, meant that I didn't have to protest: 'Oh, you shouldn't have' when I really thought 'How nice of you.' What about you, Sophie? Did you have a good time?"

Great! I'm proud of you, Kalawaka. You accepted compliments and gifts graciously. Receiving graciously is a sign of quality caring.

"Thank you, Soph," said Kalawaka. And with that he yawned and fell fast asleep.

I do not find you by chance; I find you
by an active life of reaching out.
—Walter Tubbs

2

Initiate

THE NEXT MORNING, after a hearty breakfast that included some of Kawana's tea, Kalawaka leaned back contentedly and said to his mother, "Isn't that just like Uncle Ed not to come to the party?"

"Oh, Kalawaka!" she exclaimed. "Didn't you get the Koalagram we sent you in Los Angeles?"

"No, I didn't," Kalawaka said with a sinking sensation in the pit of his stomach. "I left there ahead of schedule. What did it say?"

"Uncle Ed died three months ago," she replied slowly.

Kalawaka's eyes grew large. He was silent for a few moments. Finally he said, "Oh, mother! Come to think of it, Aunt Mathilda just didn't seem herself last night. She was so withdrawn and—"

"Yes, she's been like that ever since Ed died. Naturally, we feel terribly sad when someone we love dies, but I'm rather worried about my sister. She's acted strangely even for a grieving koala. She quit her job and just stays in her tree all the time. You know how she loved her work, and now she really needs that job. She rarely talks to anyone and stays mostly to herself. I've never seen a koala grieve quite that way. Something just isn't right—at least not for a koala. Last night was her first time out since he died. I wish I knew what ails her."

After the initial shock wore off, great concern welled up in Kalawaka for his aunt, who seemed to be so distressed.

"Mom, I think I'll go over and see how Aunt Mathilda's doing. I really regret not speaking to her last night."

"Go ahead, Son. Maybe you can find out what's the matter."

A few minutes later, Kalawaka knocked on Aunt Mathilda's tree. "May I come up?" he asked.

Somewhat hesitant and obviously a little surprised, she called down, "Well, certainly. I mean, if you want to."

After climbing up, and discreetly leaving Sophie on the porch, Kalawaka entered and blurted, "Aunt Mathilda, I just now heard about Uncle Ed. I never received the Koalagram my parents sent me. I'm so sorry."

His aunt looked down at the floor and nodded. "It's been hard since Ed died." At that moment, a teakettle started to whistle in her kitchen. "Land sakes!" she exclaimed. "I totally forgot about that tea. Would you care for some?"

As Mathilda went out to get the tea, Kalawaka wandered about distractedly, eventually looking out the front window. Sophie, he noticed, had started up on her own. *That's odd,* he thought. *I wonder if I accidentally switched her power on, trying to get her up the tree.* He read the message she had flashed on her screen.

Good work, Kalawaka! Quality caring means initiating.

O divine Master, grant that I may seek
not so much to be consoled as to
console; to be understood as to
understand; to be loved as to love.

—St. Francis of Assisi

3

Focus on Others' Needs

WHILE MATHILDA WAS FIXING THE TEA, Kalawaka pondered Sophie's message. "I wonder what we'll end up talking about," he said softly to himself. Then he smiled ruefully. "I know what I'd like to talk about: me and my trip."

But he asked himself, "What would be the quality caring thing to do? Whose needs am I here to meet?"

Of course he knew the answer. His thoughts were interrupted when Aunt Mathilda returned with the teapot and two cups of steamy eucalyptus tea. Kalawaka looked at his aunt; she looked at him, and started to cry. He reached over and gently held her paw, saying nothing. After she cried awhile, she began to talk and continued for almost an hour, nonstop. Her sorrows and heartaches came tumbling out.

But the more she talked, the less depressed she sounded. He thought he could detect just a glimmer of a lighter mood. As Kalawaka said good-bye and climbed down the tree (no small feat with Sophie under one arm), Sophie started to click furiously.

"Not now, Sophie, I've got to be careful."

When he reached the bottom, he set Sophie on a soft bed of moss and looked at the message she flashed on her screen:

Kalawaka, you are showing great aptitude in this business of quality caring. Not only did you initiate the caring visit, you then showed your grasp of what quality caring is all about by focusing on your aunt's needs rather than on your own needs.

"Thanks Sophie. I was tempted for a moment there, but it seemed pretty obvious that this was Aunt Mathilda's time, not mine."

In truth, people can make time for
what they choose to do; it is not really
the time but the will that is lacking.

—Sir John Lubbock

4

Make Time for Others

AFTER THE HUSTLE AND BUSTLE of his first days at home began to die away, Kalawaka still faced a formidable stack of mail and other chores crying out for his attention. One afternoon, just as he became engrossed in his task, he heard a voice on his side of the tree.

"Who can that be?" he said to himself, leaning over the edge of his branch and looking down.

It was Canberra, his nephew. Now Canberra was a sweet kid, but his questions never stopped. Moreover, he had a singular knack for showing up at the most inopportune moments.

"Hello, there, Canberra! What can I do for you?" Kalawaka called out.

Climbing the tree, Canberra replied, "Well, actually, I was kind of hoping that you might be able to talk with me about caring. I mean, everyone is talking about your trip and about all you learned, and I want to learn how to do quality caring too." Catching sight of Kalawaka's room, Canberra exclaimed, "Wow! What a mess!"

"Yes," Kalawaka agreed, grimacing slightly. "This is the first chance I've had to catch up with my correspondence and other such things." As Kalawaka surveyed the huge task before him, Canberra asked, a little doubtfully, "Do you think you could find time to talk—sometime?"

Kalawaka thought for a few seconds and said, "How about tonight after dinner?"

· "That's great, I'll see you then, Uncle Kalawaka!" Canberra shouted as he scampered down the tree.

"Did I ever have that much energy?" Kalawaka wondered aloud.

I don't know about that, but you certainly are becoming a quality carer par excellence.

Kalawaka jumped. "Why Sophie! I didn't know you were listening."

Kalawaka, do you realize what you've done? You made time for another koala. That's a sign of a caring koala if there ever was one. You know, we call it quality caring, but maybe we should really call it Koalaty Caring!

"Oh, Sophie," Kalawaka muttered, "I didn't know computers could come up with bad puns. Thanks for the compliment, though."

The first duty of love is
to listen.

—Paul Tillich

5

Listen

THE REST OF THE AFTERNOON, Kalawaka was lost to the
world. Project after project was brought to slow, pains-
taking completion and still more work appeared. He was
so immersed in his tasks that his mother had to call him
twice.

"Dinner is getting cold! Kalawaka? Are you coming
down?"

"Oh! Yes, mother."

Kalawaka was not very good company at dinner that
night. But his parents understood. After all, they had
seen the condition of his room. Just as Kalawaka was
finishing his meal, still preoccupied with cleaning up
the mess, the doorbell rang. It was Canberra.

Kalawaka despaired. He had forgotten all about his nephew! "But a promise is a promise," Kalawaka told himself.

They sat down in his room and Canberra began to tell Kalawaka all about what he planned to do when he started traveling. But Kalawaka was having a hard time concentrating on Canberra. His eyes continually caught sight of this or that unfinished job. Once or twice he almost forgot that Canberra was there. After struggling for a few more minutes, Kalawaka saw a light glowing over Canberra's left shoulder.

Sophie had started up on her own again and in big letters across the screen Kalawaka could read:

A quality carer LISTENS!

Kalawaka thought to himself, *Yes, Sophie, you are absolutely right.* He turned to Canberra. "Canberra, let me share one of the most important things I learned about caring on my trip. To give quality caring, I must learn to listen to others. Now, there's a whole lot more to listening than just sitting back and looking interested in what another koala is saying. Listening means that I sift the other koala's words carefully to hear the feelings behind them. In other words, I listen for what *isn't* said as well as what *is* said. I help the other koala express his or her thoughts and feelings by repeating what I think the person meant. I explain what I perceive the koala to be saying and check to see if it's what the koala really meant. Listening, Canberra, is a lot of work. It might even involve concentrating on someone at times when I'd rather concentrate on something else."

Well, Canberra really listened to his uncle for a while, and then Kalawaka stopped speaking and really listened to Canberra, and so it went for the rest of the evening. Kalawaka didn't think about his work anymore. He was giving all his attention to Canberra.

Great works are performed not
by strength but by perseverance.
—Samuel Johnson

6

Follow-up

THE NEXT DAY DAWNED BRIGHT AND CLEAR. Kalawaka rose
with the sun and set about finishing up the remaining
projects from the day before. "It's amazing how much
work I can plow through in the early morning," he com-
mented to his mother as he sat down to breakfast some
hours later. "I still have things left to do, but—"

"But what, dear?"

"I was thinking about going over to see Aunt Mathilda
again."

"I'm sure she'd appreciate it, dear. Your work will still
be here when you get back," his mother said, smiling.

Within the hour, Kalawaka was knocking at Aunt
Mathilda's tree. "Hello there, Aunt Mathilda!" he shouted. "Mind if I climb up?"

"Kalawaka! How delightful!"

After he reached her living room branch, Mathilda said, "So many people dropped by to see me right away after Ed died, but I haven't seen them since. It's as if they forgot I'm here. But you didn't forget. It's so nice to see you."

"Auntie, I'm glad I decided to stop by. I thought about you a lot this past week."

Their conversation picked up about where it had left off before. After talking about sundry things for a while, Mathilda said: "Kalawaka, I've never told anyone this before . . ." She began to cry, and big, salty koala tears ran down her fur. "You see, several years ago your Uncle Ed and I just weren't getting along very well. And . . . I met a koala who lived in the next grove. Well, he knew just what to do to make a lonely koala feel . . . not so lonely—if you take my meaning."

Kalawaka nodded slowly.

"It didn't last long. Ed and I managed to work things out. In fact, I had nearly forgotten about it until Ed died. Then all of a sudden I felt so guilty. I never told him. He never knew."

Mathilda was crying in earnest now. Kalawaka sat beside her, held her paw, and let her cry to her heart's content. After some time the sobs grew quieter. They talked some more and Kalawaka could sense, ever so slightly, that simply sharing her feelings with another koala had helped to ease the pain.

As he got up to leave, Kalawaka gave his aunt a hug and said, "If you'd like, I'll stop by again."

"Oh, Kalawaka, that would be wonderful. How about next Tuesday for tea?"

"Tuesday it is!" he said and climbed down the tree.

Later that day, after Kalawaka told Sophie all that had happened, she said:

You did a very caring thing today, Kalawaka. You followed up by visiting your aunt again. You know, she'd never have been able to begin to work through all those feelings in a single visit. Healing takes time. A quality carer follows up on caring encounters. Well done!

There is so much good in the worst of
us, and so much bad in the best of us,
that it behooves all of us not to talk
about the rest of us.
— Robert Louis Stevenson

7

Keep Confidences

As Kalawaka climbed the family tree, his mother
greeted him. "Well, from the smile on your face, you
and Mathilda must have had a good talk."

"Yes, I think we did. It was good to talk with her."

"Say, Kalawaka, could you help me with the dishes?
I need to get to a school board meeting. You know how
I feel about education for our young koalas."

While they did the dishes, Kalawaka's mother asked,
"So what did you and Aunt Mathilda talk about?"

"Oh, we talked about old times and Uncle Ed, you
know—"

"Did she say what's been bothering her so much since
then?"

Kalawaka stopped dead in his tracks and almost
dropped a dish. He knew that his aunt wouldn't mind

if he discussed in a general way that they had talked about Ed and her feelings. But his aunt would be horrified if he told anyone the specifics about her guilt. He said, "Well, Mom, one of the things I've learned is that quality caring means keeping confidences when another koala shares them with you."

"Oh, but she's my sister—"

"I know, Mom. It's just that I prefer keeping my time together with Aunt Mathilda as a private treasure. I hope you understand."

She smiled. "Well, I guess I do. Thank you for helping with the dishes, and for teaching me something about the importance of keeping confidences."

"You're welcome, Mom."

> But Divine Gift-love in the man
> enables him to love what is not
> naturally lovable: lepers, criminals,
> enemies, morons, the sulky, the
> superior, and the sneering.
> —C. S. Lewis

8

Care for the "Unlovable"

KALAWAKA HAD ALWAYS GOTTEN ALONG quite well with most koalas. Ever since his school days he had been popular. Most koalas liked him and he had many friends. In fact, there was really only one koala among all his acquaintances who absolutely rubbed Kalawaka the wrong way: Standley Kawae. Standley and Kalawaka had grown up as next-door neighbors, and Standley was what most koalas would consider a nerd. Not that his personality was abrasive, but Standley just wasn't too terribly "with it." Moreover, he never seemed to do anything right.

Standley always regarded Kalawaka as a close friend (much to Kalawaka's chagrin). But the only things that they had in common were living next to each other and being the same age. Frankly, Kalawaka always felt Standley was a threat to his popularity.

Standley just seemed to ignore all the negative messages that Kalawaka sent his way, never accepting the fact that his "friend" was a rather poor friend, if a friend at all. It seems that "hope springs eternal in the koala's breast," and so Standley continued to pretend that, despite the evidence, Kalawaka was truly his friend.

Somewhere along the line, Standley had fallen a year behind Kalawaka in school, and Kalawaka was greatly relieved. Now, a year after Kalawaka's graduation, Standley was graduating. To celebrate the occasion, Standley's parents were throwing a party, and Kalawaka and his parents were invited. Naturally his mother accepted for them all.

When Kalawaka heard the news, he was somewhat perturbed. "Mom, how could you possibly have said yes? You didn't even ask me!"

"Now, Kalawaka, Standley thinks quite highly of you and I know you wouldn't want to disappoint him."

Kalawaka gulped. "Oh, no!" he groaned under his breath and climbed up to his branch in a huff. No sooner had he reached his room when Sophie started whizzing and whirring.

KALAWAKA!

"What?" Kalawaka virtually shouted back.

SIT DOWN AND LISTEN UP! A quality carer reaches out to the unlovable. This is the first time since we met that you have acted like being a quality carer doesn't matter.

"But, Sophie, you don't know him!"

I don't have to, Kalawaka. You don't have to pretend he is your best friend if he isn't. But he is a koala—a koala with fears and needs and desires and questions and ambitions and a hundred other feelings pulsing through him. You don't have to be his bosom buddy; you only have to care enough to affirm his koalahood. And who knows? You might end up liking him more than you think. Let's face it, Kal, you haven't given him much of a chance.

Kalawaka hung his head. Of course Sophie was right. He hadn't even been treating Standley civilly. Kalawaka knew that quality caring required that he be accepting and affirm Standley as a koala of value.

"Okay, Soph, I hear you."

With that she shut off and the branch grew very silent. As Kalawaka tossed and turned that night, he was feeling some guilt—some very realistic guilt. He awoke the next morning prepared to go to the party and put into practice all the quality caring he knew.

Many parent koalas came to Standley's party, but only a handful of koalas his own age. Most of the young koalas stayed together in a small group, away from their parents and away from Standley. When Kalawaka arrived, he headed straight for Standley.

"Hi, Standley. Congratulations!"

Standley was floored. "Uh . . . thanks, Kalawaka. Thanks for coming, too."

"How does it feel? Being out of school I mean. You know, ready to face the real world?"

Standley was even more astounded. No one had ever asked him how he felt about anything before, especially not any of his peers. They seemed not to care in the least how he felt.

"Well, Kalawaka, to be honest I feel a little—no, a whole lot—afraid. Who knows? I may be as big a failure out there in the real world as I was in school."

"How is that?" Kalawaka asked. Standley took a deep breath and started talking about his feelings of the past, present, and future. As he was sharing, a strange thing started to happen. One by one, a few of the other young koalas drifted toward them and awkwardly found a place in the conversation. When Kalawaka finally said good-bye to Standley and left with his parents, Standley was still talking with the others.

As Kalawaka walked home that night with his parents, he thanked his mother for accepting the invitation. As he climbed his branch, he said, "You know, Mom, Standley's really not so bad after all."

Life has taught me to forgive much,
but to seek forgiveness still more.
                    —Otto von Bismarck

9

Apologize

As KALAWAKA WAS INDULGING HIMSELF in a nostalgic look through his old high school yearbooks, he suddenly exclaimed: "By George! You know I haven't seen my good friend Cobber since the week after we graduated, when he moved to Sir Colin McKenzie Sanctuary. Here I've traveled all over the world and haven't even made time to see him!"

Right away Kalawaka made arrangements with Cobber, typed a quick "good-bye" into Sophie, and traveled to the next province to visit him. And what a wonderful visit it was! They talked eagerly of times past and mutual friends, relishing the sweet sadness of nostalgia that suddenly engulfs koalas as they realize they've been out of school for an entire year. The time seemed to pass far too quickly, but many good things do come to an end. They said a cheerful good-bye and Kalawaka was on his way.

All in all, it was an absolutely perfect visit. That's why the next event seemed so odd. As Kalawaka neared his home, he grew quite hungry, but he still had a good hour to travel. He debated whether or not to stop, or just keep going and eat at home. Hunger won out. He stopped at a fast-food restaurant.

Now, it felt as if he had to wait in line forever, and koalas can be notoriously grumpy when they're hungry, so it's not all that surprising that Kalawaka was down-right irritable when he finally placed his order. "Give me a gum leaf patty—rare—to go," he said impatiently.

"It'll be just a minute, sir."

It was much more than a minute before Kalawaka got his patty, but he was so happy to get some food that he didn't mind. When he took a bite of it, though, he shouted "Yuck!" spitting it out. The patty was almost burnt. Now he was really angry. Kalawaka marched back up to the counter and proceeded to yell, holler, stamp his feet, and chew out the poor fellow who had handed him the patty.

Kalawaka made such a scene that the manager ran up front to see what the problem was. The manager tried to soothe Kalawaka's bristling fur, but to no avail. One very upset koala left the fast-food joint with the slender satisfaction of having yelled at the poor young koala who waited on him.

At home that night, he began to feel uncomfortable about his behavior. He tried to dismiss his thoughts and get some sleep, but by and large he spent a restless night. Visions of that young koala's hurt face kept creeping into his mind. At first he fought with himself, saying things like, "He deserved it for giving me an overcooked patty." But it was hopeless. Kalawaka knew he was wrong. The more he thought about it, the more guilty he felt. He realized that even if his complaint were legitimate, his response was uncalled for. Furthermore, he had unloaded his anger on the poor lad who had sold him the burger, not the cook who had made it. There was no way the young koala at the counter could have known that the patty was ruined. Awareness of that fact made him flush hotly under his fur coat. "How unfair I was! I was wrong—very wrong." Kalawaka resolved to go back to the restaurant and apologize to the young koala.

Kalawaka was in luck. When he arrived, the place was mostly empty, and the young koala was standing there, ready to wait on someone. "Sir, I'm so sorry about yesterday," the young koala began nervously when he saw Kalawaka.

"No, I'm the one who's sorry, and I came back to tell you how wrong I was."

"But, it shouldn't have been overcooked—"

"I agree. But my behavior was still inappropriate. I'm very sorry."

After a pause, the young koala said slowly, "Well, thank you, sir."

"Since I'm here, I might as well have a sandwich. How about another gum leaf patty?" Kalawaka said.

"Coming right up!"

As Kalawaka was enjoying his patty, the manager came up and said, "Mind if I have a seat?"

"No, by all means, sit down."

"I want to thank you for coming back to apologize to the kid. It was his first day yesterday, and that whole scene really upset him. I had a big job convincing him to come back to work today."

Kalawaka lowered his head. "I didn't know."

"Please don't worry. The kid was lucky it was a koala like you with enough character to come back and apologize. And just look at him now. You've made his day. Thanks again." The manager got up and left.

Christ said "Love your enemies." But
what do you do when you discover
your greatest enemy to be yourself?
—Viktor Frankl

10

Forgive Yourself

EVEN THOUGH HIS LATEST EXPERIENCE at the leaf-patty joint was very positive, Kalawaka felt somewhat depressed all the way home. He kept repeating to himself, "I'm supposed to be someone who knows what quality caring is all about. How could I have behaved like that in the first place?" In fact, these were the words he muttered as he climbed up into his room when he got home that night. Suddenly Sophie flashed:

What did you say?

"I said, 'I'm supposed to know what quality caring is all about, so I shouldn't have behaved so horribly in the first place.'" Kalawaka went on to tell her the whole grim story from beginning to end.

After hearing him out, she replied:

I see your point. But you apologized didn't you?

"Yes."

You said you were sorry and you meant it, right?

"I sure did."

Didn't you say that the lad forgave you and he's feeling okay now?

"It certainly looked that way."

Mm. Do you know what's going on here? There's someone else you need to forgive.

"Tell me, Sophie, and I'll go right back."

You don't have to go anywhere.

"What do you mean?"

You, Kalawaka. You need to forgive yourself. Kalawaka, right now you are your own worst enemy.

Kalawaka almost laughed, but thought better of it at the last moment. "Okay, Sophie, here goes."

He walked over to the mirror, looked at the chubby face staring back at him, and said, "Kalawaka, I did wrong. I am sorry." He then shouted over his shoulder to Sophie: "What next?"

Tell yourself you're forgiven.

Kalawaka looked back into the mirror and hesitatingly said, "Kalawaka, it's okay. I . . . I. . . ." He turned around and looked at Sophie. "This is hard to do."

I know, Kalawaka. Say it anyway.

Again staring into the mirror, Kalawaka said, "I forgive you . . . er, me . . . uh, you know what I mean." Kalawaka smiled from ear to ear. He began to feel better. "Hey, Sophie! You were right. Forgiving myself was the hardest part."

Kalawaka, you really don't need to stand in front of a mirror. But you know how it's done now. You honestly confront yourself and then forgive yourself. And it may not relieve the guilt so quickly either. You may have to do it repeatedly. That's okay.

"Wow! Thanks a bundle. Forgiving yourself does give you a bit of a lift, doesn't it?"

I'm not sure exactly how it feels, Kalawaka. I'm a computer and a computer never makes a mistake. I've never had to forgive myself.

Kalawaka laughed with great delight and turned Sophie off for the night.

Touching is not only nice. It's needed.
Scientific research supports the theory
that stimulation by touch is absolutely
necessary for our physical as well as
our emotional well-being.

—Kathleen Keating

11

Touch

KALAWAKA WAS GAINING QUITE A REPUTATION for quality caring. Koalas from all over came to appreciate his caring. Take for instance what happened to his neighbors who lived three trees down the row.

Karen was rushed to the hospital (Koala General— two groves over) for surgery. Being a friend of Karen and her family and being determined to give quality caring, Kalawaka made a point of going to the hospital to pay a visit.

When Kalawaka arrived at Koala General, Karen's husband, Duke, and their children were sound asleep in the waiting area, having spent all night and much of the day with Karen. Kalawaka slipped by them, leaving them to their much-needed rest, and went in to see Karen.

"You're awake!" Kalawaka said.

"Oh! Hello, Kalawaka. Yes, I'm very much awake. I just can't seem to calm down enough to get to sleep."

The tone in her voice moved Kalawaka. He knew she was worried about the slight possibility (it was the "possibility" that scared her more than the "slight" could console her) that even though the surgery was over, she still might not fully recover.

Kalawaka reached out and grasped her paw, saying, "You sound a little frightened."

As it turned out, she was quite frightened. She was worried about her family. Who would take care of them if she died, or even while she was recovering? She was worried about the hospital bills. The whole time Karen spoke, Kalawaka held her paw and listened. The relief of sharing her burden seemed to be the very thing to relax her.

"Gee, Kalawaka," she yawned. "I didn't realize how tired I was. Thanks for stopping . . ." She drifted off to sleep.

When Kalawaka left her room, he found that Duke and the kids (Sarah and Jason) had awakened.

"Kalawaka!" Duke exclaimed. "It's good to see you. I didn't see you come in." Despite his cheerful greeting, Kalawaka could sense how worried he was.

Kalawaka walked over and put his paw on Duke's shoulder. "I'll say you didn't. All three of you were sound asleep when I arrived."

Duke smiled. "It has been a long day."

"Yes, you all must be exhausted."

Kalawaka knew that Duke would never think of letting the kids see how really worried he was. There was no need to do so. In all likelihood everything was going to turn out all right in the end, and they were frightened enough anyway over being separated from their mother. "Look, Duke, Karen just dropped off to sleep, but I am sure you would still like to spend some time with her alone. Why don't I take these two downstairs and treat them to some eucalyptus ice-cream cones?"

Duke smiled and nodded. "Would you kids like that?"

"Yeah!" chimed Sarah and Jason in unison.

Later on, as Kalawaka was sitting with his cone, Sarah sat on his lap and leaned against him. Jason leaned against Kalawaka's left arm and Kalawaka put his arm around him.

A sense of discovery came over Kalawaka. There was a very important lesson to be learned about caring from all this touching. After returning the kids to Duke, Kalawaka put this question to Sophie: "To touch or not to touch?" Sophie flashed back:

Kalawaka, you struck a gold mine. Since we are here in the hospital, why not hook me up to the big computer here? We're very compatible. That way I can have the hospital printer print out my answer for you.

Well, Kalawaka did just that, and this was Sophie's response:

I will answer your question with several of my own:

1. *Are you comfortable with touching?* If you aren't, then don't do it. A touch communicates as surely as a word. You don't want to send a wrong message. To touch with reservation is to communicate distance and lack of concern. To touch uneasily is to communicate discomfort. When you touch because you think you "have to," your touch only communicates "I'd rather not be doing this." The flip side of the coin is this: To touch with concern communicates love; to touch with ease communicates comfort in the other's presence; to touch with

freedom communicates that you are present because you choose to be.

2. *Is the other koala comfortable with touching?* Remember, you are present to meet the other koala's needs—not your own. If the other koala is uncomfortable with touching, physical contact of any sort, even the best-intentioned touch will probably be misunderstood. When you see that a koala shies away from physical contact, don't force it!

3. *Will the touching further the caring process?* Kalawaka, I can think of a situation where you would be very comfortable touching and so would the other koala, but the touching would not be for caring reasons—if you know what I mean. Frankly, Kalawaka, some kinds of touching could endanger a caring relationship. I'm no prude, but be careful not to confuse different kinds of touching. Always ask yourself the three questions before touching in a caring situation, Kalawaka. If the answers are yes, then by all means, go ahead! But, if you have any doubts, don't touch. Got it?

Now that response just knocked Kalawaka off his feet. It seemed so obvious. Of course! He would never have held Karen's paw, put his arm on Duke's shoulder, or held the kids if he were uncomfortable with it. Had any of them been uncomfortable with touching, or if it wouldn't have helped, he wouldn't have done it either.

Very pleased with his new discovery, Kalawaka unhooked Sophie from the hospital's computer, gave her a warm hug, and headed for home.

Be at peace with yourself first and
then you will be able to
bring peace to others.
—Thomas à Kempis

12

Care for Yourself

KALAWAKA HAD BEEN HOME for a couple of months, busy putting all his new knowledge about caring into practice. But one morning he started to feel slightly ill. "No matter," he said to himself. "I am a koalaty carer (he had adopted Sophie's terminology), and no sickness is going to get in my way!" So, swallowing hard, he slowly climbed down his tree and went about his rounds. He stopped in on Aunt Mathilda who was doing well—"almost back to herself," the neighbors said—and then he trotted over to visit Karen and Duke and their family. Karen had been home from the hospital for several days, and she so enjoyed his visits that she had asked Kalawaka to come over again. Then there was Canberra. Kalawaka promised to spend some more time sharing with him about quality caring. Oh, yes; Kalawaka had also planned to eat lunch with Standley.

When Kalawaka climbed into his home tree early that afternoon, he collapsed on the sofa.

"Kalawaka, you look horrible!" his mother exclaimed. "Stay right where you are until I come back with a thermometer." Wouldn't you know it? Our friend had quite a fever. He was so busy caring that he had run himself ragged.

"Kalawaka, I think you should go right up to bed and stay there until you're better," his mother said.

"Mom, I can't do that. I have to see Mrs. Brisbane this afternoon and—"

"Kalawaka, you know I can't make you stay at home, but if you don't take care of yourself, all those needy koalas are going to have to come see you—in the hospital. I know you don't want that."

After a feeble argument, Kalawaka finally gave in and said, "You're right, as usual, Mom." After he settled into his bed upstairs, he said, "Here's a list of koalas I was supposed to see this afternoon. Could you contact them for me and explain that I'm a little under the weather?"

"I'd be happy to do that, Son," his mom said as she descended the branch.

As Kalawaka drifted off to sleep, he thought he saw a light on the far side of his room. It was Sophie, and she was flashing him this message:

A quality carer cares for self, looking out for his or her own feelings and overall health while caring for others. If he or she doesn't do so, there will be one less quality carer. GET SOME REST!

With that, Sophie's screen went dark again.

"Thanks again, old friend," Kalawaka mumbled and fell into a deep sleep.

Make a joyful noise to the LORD,
all the earth.

—Psalm 100:1

13

Enjoy

A FEW WEEKS LATER, as his caring became a more balanced part of his total life, Kalawaka decided to take a day off to be alone. He packed a lunch and climbed a large hill (a small mountain to koalas) just west of the eucalyptus grove, taking Sophie with him.

The day was balmy. The sun was warm, and a delicious breeze kept it from being too hot. As Kalawaka looked down on the quiet grove that was his home, his thoughts took him back to another "hill" he had experienced before—the mountain at Delphi. "How my life has changed since then," he said to himself. He began to reflect. Learning to be a quality carer had transformed his whole life.

Before, I never really had the joy of listening to what other koalas were saying. I was always impatient, waiting until it would be polite for me to talk. Now I can listen, really listen to others, and when I've heard them out, I discover they are priceless treasures. Before, I worried about how to act so I could impress other koalas. Now, I can be myself—plainly and simply—without concerning myself about masks. Before, I thought helping others was something I ought to do. Now, I think of it as something I love to do, and so I consciously set aside time to do it.

"Sophie, my fine and thoughtful friend," Kalawaka sang out, "tell me what I've learned since I got home."

You can call this "Kalawaka's Guide to Quality Caring." If you are a quality carer, you will:
- RECEIVE GRACIOUSLY
- INITIATE
- FOCUS ON OTHERS' NEEDS
- MAKE TIME FOR OTHERS
- LISTEN
- FOLLOW-UP
- KEEP CONFIDENCES
- CARE FOR THE "UNLOVABLE"
- APOLOGIZE
- FORGIVE YOURSELF
- TOUCH
- CARE FOR YOURSELF

Last, but not least, you are learning right now that A QUALITY CARER ENJOYS. Enjoy yourself, Kalawaka. Enjoy your life. Enjoy your caring.

Well, these musings led Kalawaka to greater and greater appreciation of what quality caring is and the power it has to change lives. He was so full of joy that he couldn't refrain from laughing. And he laughed and he laughed.

"A quality carer, above and beyond everything else, enjoys laughing," he said to himself. "Quality caring gives meaning, purpose, and direction to life, true enough, but it also brings joy in the midst of hard work." And so our story draws to a close. We take leave of our marsupial friend. But I hope he's hooked you on quality caring, too. If he has, this will be . . .

THE BEGINNING